FEAR IS NOT AN OPTION

To Tracey

Michele Anstead

MICHELE ANSTEAD

JOANS ISLAND PUBLISHING

FEAR IS NOT AN OPTION

Copyright © 2015 by Michele Anstead

Published by Joans Island Publishing

ALL RIGHTS RESERVED

Without limiting the rights under copyright reserved above, no part of this publication may be reproduced, stored in or introduced into retrieval system, or transmitted in any form or by and means (electronic, mechanical, photocopying, recording or otherwise), without the prior written permission of both the copyright owner and the above publisher of this book.

Manufactured in Canada

Printed in the United States

Library and Archives Canada Cataloguing in Publication

Anstead, Michele, author
   Fear is not an option / Michele Anstead.

ISBN 978-0-9939654-0-1 (paperback)

      1. Anstead, Michele. 2. Adult child abuse victims--Canada--
Biography. I. Title.

HV6626.54.C3A57 2015   362.76092   C2015-905290-4

Some names and identifying details have been changed to protect the privacy of individuals. I have tried to recreate events, locales and conversations from my memories of them. In order to maintain their anonymity in some instances I have changed the names of individuals and places, I may have changed some identifying characteristics and details such as physical properties, occupations and places of residence.

Cover Illustration by Michele Anstead

Editing by Elizabeth Ridley

Visit Joans Island Publishing on the web at:

http://www.joansislandpublishing.com:

DEDICATION

To my beloved son Tyler, who came into my life at just the right time.

My days were done, my life almost over,

And there you were, my savior, my son.

I made you a promise when you were born,

You would have no pain,

I would protect you from all evil,

Be there for you whenever you needed me,

And most of all love you with all my heart and soul.

I hope I have not disappointed you. I truly did my best.

This is my story of all I endured,

to keep my promise to you and why.

For my loving, angelic sister Jennifer, without your belief in me, your kind heart and soul, I would not have felt worthy to live. Do not change who you are. Thank you forever and always.

To my soul mate, Rick, for listening to me cry out of the blue during the months while I relived my life story in order to write this book. For showing me that not all men are "assholes". And most of all, for loving me without judgment.

CONTENTS

ACKNOWLEDGMENTS

Anthony Robbins, for inspiring me to be my best, change my state and never let anything hold me down.

Elizabeth Ridley (Editor), for her knowledge and patience when editing my book.

Unknown Woman, we stole your purse near the Dundas Subway station sometime between 1978-1980. When you caught us, you asked us why. We told you we were hungry and lived on the streets. You bought us dinner and gave us $20 and your number and said if we ever needed help to call you. I have never forgotten that night. Your kindness touched my heart and I never did that again and have always paid it forward.

For all the negative people in the world, thank you for wallowing in your own self-pity. You give me strength and the will to do everything in my power "NOT to be like you".

INTRODUCTION

I truly believe in my heart that everything happens for a reason. Although it was extremely difficult for me, while writing this book, to revisit the most painful areas of my life, I knew it was necessary to do so in order to bring my story of hope, inspiration, and triumph to readers. I sincerely hope that sharing my experiences will help others to look more deeply into their own lives, and to find forgiveness and the strength to move on, no matter what adversity they face. Throughout the book and throughout my life it was always my belief system, good or bad, that steered me in the next direction. It either held me back or moved me forward. It was the catalyst for all my actions.

I was born with a deep-rooted belief that I would face life-threatening challenges and constant change. Unfortunately, my premonition proved to be true as I struggled through abuse, deprivation, abandonment, addiction, incarceration, and loss. Studies have shown that the first seven years of your life have a great impact on who you become. If that is so, and given the events of my first seven years, how am I still alive today? And not just alive, but thriving and continuing to believe that I am here to serve a greater purpose and that all of the horrible things I have been through happened in order for me to help others. I'm not sure I can answer the question of how or why I survived, but once a smile comes upon my face and the blood starts to pump throughout my body, I gain an enormous strength and know that somehow I will win.

Winning, in this context, means surviving in a world full of pain and suffering. Winning is finding love in some of the smallest things. It's holding on to happiness as you glide to the next journey in your life. Winning is never giving up. It is making a difference in someone's life, even if only for a moment. Winning is knowing that they cannot pull you down no matter how hard they try. Winning is not based on gaining money or material things. Winning means finding inner peace and knowing that you are doing all that is necessary to fulfill the promise of your life.

Although this is a true story I have changed the names and some minor details in order to protect the identities of people close to me and also to protect those who may not be ready to have their own faults and indiscretions publicly exposed.

What follows is the story of a young girl who needed a whole lifetime to understand and accept the true meaning of love.

CHAPTER ONE

FIRST IMPRESSIONS

Where shall I start? It is spring 1964. A second girl, Michele, is born out of wedlock. Hearts and souls shouted out, "Not another girl," and the infant girl screamed back at the top of her lungs as if to say, "I am here." This is how my life began.

After my being the baby of the family for 19 months, out came the beloved boy. Both of my parents had done mostly fighting and quarreling throughout their relationship, and now the savior was born and a light of hope shone, or so they thought. By the time I was four years old my parents had split up many times. Oh but their love was so powerful--unbelievably powerful. You've heard of a love-hate relationship. Well, this was it in spades.

I can't tell you too much about the love part except what I saw in their eyes during and after many years when they spoke of each other. They would light up like a bright white full moon in amidst a pitch black sky full of stars. That is the only way I can explain the deepness of it. The air completely filled with warm softness that seemed to hug you, yet at a distance appeared as if to hold strong in knowing it was over and could not possibly last. I must tell you about the bad stuff so you can understand my strength and determination even when all odds were against me from the start.

Let's talk about my mom and dad. Meigan, my mom, was born in Guyana, South America in 1932, one of seven children. When Meigan was eleven years old her mom passed away during childbirth. The children were left to be raised by their father. This was extremely uncommon, especially in Guyana, back in those days. Aside from the fact that Meigan's father was an alcoholic who only got worse after his wife died, he was all they had left. It was far too difficult for him to take care of seven children on his own while working, and drinking the rest of the time, so he decided to send the five girls to a Catholic Hospital School run by the nuns. Part of the school was an orphanage and the other part was for paying children, which Meigan's father had done. They were allowed one weekend visit per month and then on holidays. The two boys were kept at home with their father.

You must have heard the stories about nuns or you may have even experienced them first hand yourself. I am sure that God did not put these people here to make us suffer. That could not have been His intention. Somehow the nuns took it upon themselves to discipline the children in not-so-kind ways. They would often beat them with sticks and various objects. The nuns would lock them in solitary in dark rooms for many hours and sometimes days. Meigan was feisty; she had taken on the responsibility of protecting her brothers and sisters while putting fear behind her.

One day Meigan's younger sister Leslie hurt her leg and was placed in the infirmary. Meigan was worried and concerned and wanted to see her. The nuns refused. Meigan being the pig-headed person she was would not take no for an answer. So she escaped from her room and climbed a big barbed wire fence to go see Leslie. After being caught and receiving much punishment she began working on an escape plan that she would soon no longer need.

By the time Meigan turned fourteen she had lost her father to a brain tumor. Now the children were all alone. Once their father died there was no longer any money to pay for their schooling; not that Meigan wanted to remain there anyway. In response to this and with nowhere else to turn, one of her aunts decided to step up to the plate and let the children live with her. This situation turned out to be worse than living with the nuns as the aunt was quite mean to the children. They were beaten and teased while being made to sleep on the hard floor with no bed. Leftovers from the table were fed to Meigan and her siblings as if they were dogs. They were treated as second-class citizens but without any parents left they had no option but to withstand this treatment until it was time to leave.

Meigan, looking to escape this wretched life she was in, found herself spending the night with a man who would use her for his own pleasure. Not too long after that she became pregnant with his child and that same man chose not to take responsibility for his actions. Now you must understand how difficult it was back then. It was during a time when a pregnant woman who was not wed was a disgrace to society, not to mention the fact that she was only seventeen years old at the time. Meigan was shunned wherever she went, spit on and talked about behind her back. Although she was tough it was still very difficult for her to continue to walk with her head held high each and every day, but she did.

Meigan was a very attractive woman, five-foot-one and a hundred and three pounds with a stunning similarity to Queen Elizabeth. People came up to her and told her many times how much she looked like the Queen. This was her prime years and now she had the glow of pregnancy shining through. So much that she caught one man's eye. He was twenty-two years older than her and had money, a job and could provide her with the security she needed. Hooking up with him could certainly alleviate some of the pressures of societal condemnation and might afford her some reprieve in the end. So when he asked her to marry him she willfully said yes without any thought.

Now don't get me wrong; I do think they had some kind of a bond which ran along the lines of more of a father-daughter relationship, so to speak. She respected him and was eternally grateful that he helped her escape her life as a nomad. He accepted her baby girl, Jessie, who was born months later, as his own. Although things were comfortable in their relationship they knew Guyana was not a safe place, with many riots going on during which people would be choked and robbed on the streets, so they decided to go to Canada. They had heard that Canada was a great country and provided many services to their citizens, unlike Guyana. So this must be the place to be, they thought, and off they went.

It wasn't until several years later, long after they were settled in Canada and fairly comfortable with their lives, that Meigan became pregnant again. Although their connection was more of a friendship they did entertain some of their sexual desires and that was how their son Paul was born. As we all know a relationship based simply on friendship and not true love never really lasts unless the parties involved continue to sacrifice their true selves.

Meigan was not prepared to do that forever and would soon venture out on her own. With her friends at her side she would frequent the clubs at night. She knew her much-older husband was tired and worn out and was not interested in these activities so she left him behind.

This is where she met Fred, my dad, at the El Mocombo in Toronto. It was an instant connection. They both loved dancing and the excitement of the night life. Although when Meigan first met Fred she wasn't much of a drinker, she soon caved to the likes of alcohol. Fred was a tall, well-built man who looked like Elvis Presley in his prime. He was polite and romantic and with his sexy British accent Meigan fell hard and soon they were inseparable.

One major thing that later put a strain on their relationship was her drinking. Fred was accustomed to drinking due to his British upbringing and the commonality of pubs as a part of life and with his large stature he just seemed to be able to handle it better than Meigan. He was more of a happy drinker and Meigan was the opposite. She became violent and aggressive, releasing all of her childhood frustrations out on Fred and whoever stood in her way. This would later lead to more hardship but with casualties that we will talk about later.

By the time I was three there had been so much violence surrounding my young life. To start with, my parents, or at least my mother, really wanted a boy. They had already had a baby girl together named Jennifer; they called her Jenny for short, born three and a half years earlier. So you could interpret that as I wasn't really wanted from birth. At least I did; I somehow felt this subconsciously. Every day was spent trying to prove myself, especially after my brother Mason was born. I was pushed aside like a piece of trash at the side of the road. Inside Meigan felt that having a son would somehow fix her relationship with Fred. Like I said there would be casualties in the crossfire.

The drinking and violence continued night after night. When Meigan's brother and sisters participated in the partying the fights always seemed to break out. Meigan's sister Anna had a boyfriend named Giovanni who brought their own quandary to the table.

As the story goes they were all sure Giovanni had ties to the mob but no one knew for sure. He was your typical image of the mafia-style man that existed in the movies. Tall, dark-haired, broad shoulders, big hands and he usually wore a suit and dark glasses.

One day the family gathered to have some drinks as they usually did, starting early afternoon. Everyone seemed so happy, dancing and singing, telling each other how much they loved them. It was almost too good to be true. Then suddenly as their minds became cloudy with the alcohol it was as if a group of black clouds slowly moved in and began hovering over their heads.

Giovanni was very mean and abusive to Anna when he was drinking. He had previously broken one of her arms, blackened her face and eyes with the pounding force of his large hands, so much that she became blind in one eye.

Now Meigan was a feisty woman as I mentioned before, always taking the underdog under her wings and standing up for them. This night would be no different. Everyone's voices got louder to the point you could no longer hear the music in the background. Anna felt brave standing up against Giovanni while all her family was by her side. She was in his face screaming profanities. Giovanni threw Anna onto the couch and began beating her. Meigan grabbed him with uncanny power that took over her body in protection of her sister and threw him aside.

Giovanni was not impressed and grabbed Meigan's dress as she moved away. He ripped it right off of her, leaving her standing in her slip alone. Anna jumped in to protect her sister, slapping and punching Giovanni. Giovanni was not about to let this one-hundred-and-three-pound woman push him around so he clenched his fist and with all his power punched her in the face.

In the meantime Meigan asked me, three years old at the time, to go get her a knife from the drawer. I quickly obeyed for fear my mother would be hurt next. I ran to the kitchen and opened the drawer and pulled out the biggest knife I could find, which was a six-inch paring knife. Fists were flying left, right, and center as I entered the room and started to pass my mother the knife. Then from out of nowhere the woman that lived in the upstairs apartment grabbed my little wrist and squeezed it until I let go of the knife. The woman quickly ran up the stairs to hide the knife from Meigan.

Now my sister Jenny saw this and knew it was all up to her to help our mother. So she ran into the kitchen and grabbed the only knife she could see--a massive butcher knife--and passed it to our mother.

Within seconds Meigan gripped the handle and swung her arm around and slashed Giovanni across his forehead. The skin was flapping and you could see the veins pulsating while massive pools of blood spewed out of his head. We children watched frozen in our steps as such vicious acts of violence were recorded in our minds forever.

Somebody had called the police, probably one of the neighbors, after hearing the ruckus going on inside. The sound of big heavy steel-toed footsteps could be heard approaching the door. Moments later BANG! BANG! BANG! on the door and their deep serious voices announced themselves. "It's the police, open the door or we will break it in." Anna was terrified. She had tried so hard to keep everyone calm. None of it worked and now there was a man with his head cut open bleeding profusely as the police prepared to tear down the door. She knew opening the door was the only way this would stop. With only a moment's thought she opened the door. As the officers came in with their guns drawn the noise seemed to silence almost instantly.

At first glance around the room the officers knew they needed an ambulance and called right away on their radio. Anna quickly grabbed some towels out of the closet to pass to the officers in order to apply pressure on Giovanni's wound. Once the police seemed to have everything under control their eyes scanned the room and fell upon the three children. A friendlier look came from their eyes as if to give the feeling that it was going to be OK, even though they really did not know this at the time.

Once the police had some clarification of what had gone on, of course from Meigan's family's point of view, since Giovanni was outnumbered and as the saying goes, blood is thicker than water. Giovanni was taken to the station as well as Meigan for now. You see, our father was a policeman. So it was unlikely that Meigan would actually stay in jail. The police department was almost like a legal gang. There was something like an unspoken code amongst them which stated, "serve and protect our own and our families whenever possible." Even though at the time everyone seemed to come out basically unscathed, this relationship with Anna and Giovanni was not over yet.

It would be five years later that Giovanni would bring about the demise of Meigan's dear sister Anna. Anna was found kicked to death in her home. Although it was not reported in the newspaper, Meigan said that there were cigarette butts that were extinguished all over Anna's body. He had already blinded her in one eye and broke a few bones on prior incidents so this was the final straw. According to newspaper articles it would be the first time in Ontario that a Provincial Judge would sentence a man who had pleaded guilty to a charge of manslaughter since the amendment to the Criminal Code which made it legal for crimes such as manslaughter and rape to be tried in lower courts. Both crimes previously were the exclusive jurisdiction of the higher court. Giovanni was sentenced to eight years in prison.

***

The grueling night which was the beginning of the end for Anna also brought on much hardship for us children. That night my siblings and I were taken to the Children's Aid and placed in a foster home. One might say this was safer for us considering the events of the evening we had just endured. Somehow fate had other tests we needed to pass in order to survive. It was not over yet.

Initially the placement in the Children's Aid was supposed to be temporary. It was a terrifying experience after witnessing so much madness that night and then to be taken away from our parents and put in a stranger's home. In the end these were ordinary people given extraordinary power over our young lives; power that would later be used against us.

At the court hearing several weeks later the social workers, Meigan and Fred, plus we three children, were in attendance. The social workers presented their case, inferring that due to the circumstances that had previously occurred at the house they felt that Meigan was an unfit mother. In light of that the only solution for the welfare of the children was that we remain in the care of the Children's Aid and be placed in a foster home.

The judge asked about our father. Glancing over at Mr. Anstead he said, "Can you care for your children?"

"Yes," my father said with tears filling his eyes. "I would like the children to come home with me."

"Where are you living right now?"

"I am renting a room off one of my friends."

"So there would not be spare rooms for the children at your place of residence?" the judge asked.

"No, your honor," Fred replied.

The social workers spoke very highly of Fred, saying he was a policeman and seemed to care very deeply for his children. "If Mr. Anstead had suitable living arrangements we would consider recommending the children go with him. Unfortunately this is not the case at this time."

Now, this is the crazy part: the judge looked at the children and asked each one of us individually, "Who do you want to live with?" I remember this incident quite vividly as if my limbs were being torn apart. It was totally unfair; how could we choose between our parents while both were watching us intensely in the room? When the judge asked me I started to cry and said, "I want to live with both of them."

From this day forward I held on to this memory and those final words and dreamed each and every day that someday my parents would be back together.

The judge came to his decision. "I deem the mother of these children unfit and will not allow them to be returned to her. Mr. Anstead, however, seems to have shown that he is willing to care for his children; however, he does not have the means at this time. Mr. Anstead, if you can get yourself a place of your own, one with at least separate rooms for the boys and girls, then I will overturn this order and have your children returned home to you. Until such time Jennifer, Michele, and Mason will remain in the custody of the Children's Aid Society under the care of a foster home or homes."

"Please, your honor," Fred interrupted, "may I have one request?" The judge nodded for him to go ahead. "That all three children not be separated. Can you assure me that they will be placed together in the same home?" Fred pleaded. The judge then turned to the Children's Aid worker and asked that they make every effort possible not to separate the children and they agreed.

"We will meet again in six months, at which time we will review your circumstances, Mr. Anstead. In the meantime the children are to remain in the care of the Children's Aid Society." And then a bang as the judge's mallet hit the table in a demonstration of finality.

CHAPTER TWO

SECRET LIVES OF CAREGIVERS

Oh what a terrible day that was for me. Too young to really understand what was going on, all I knew was something was not right and that the parents I knew and loved were being taken away. Maybe it was my fault. "I should have picked one parent over the other but I couldn't," I thought. "What will happen to us now? Maybe all the times I misbehaved I am now being punished." All these thoughts raced through my young mind. Well of course there was no one to validate any of this so I needed to create my own story.

With my father's help and persistence I was able to be placed in a foster home together with my brother and sister. At least I could feel some form of safety knowing my siblings were with me to help me through it. Unfortunately not only were we all quite young: Jenny, seven; Mason, three; and me, turning four, we could not always be together every second.

One day when Jenny was in school the foster father, we will call him "Mr. Smith" for this purpose, called me into his room to play a game. He called it "Blind man's bluff." I was thrilled at first to be chosen to play this game, unknowing of what was to come. As I entered the door to a small room there was a double bed with the head board on the left wall. The door opened to the right and rested against the other wall. Along the wall at the bottom of the bed was a long short dresser about the same length as the bed. Lying on top was a long crocheted doily spread across from one end to the other like a runner. Knickknacks were spread out to decorate the dresser. On each side of the bed were two end tables with lamps on top. Each end table had a top drawer to store things in.

Sitting on the side of the bed by the door was Mr. Smith, a man in his fifties, with dirty brown greasy hair all messed up like he had just woken up. He always wore a white tank top and had a big round beer belly. In actuality he was short for a man but to me he was a towering giant. At least while sitting he was more at my level.

This big burly man took my little hands in his and with a gentle soft-spoken voice whispered, "OK now, we are going to play a game. Let me tell you how it works. I am going to blindfold you and spin you around and then I am going to take an object out of this drawer beside the bed and let you feel it to guess what it is."

I was excited because I felt pretty smart and thought I could win this game.

"You would like to play this game, right?" Mr. Smith said, wide-eyed.

I replied with a smile and said, "Yes, I would like to play."

He reached for a piece of cloth that he had resting on his lap and blindfolded me. Slowly he spun me around three times and stopped me in front of him. He reached in the drawer and pulled out a pen and placed it in my hands. Right away I knew what this was and shouted, "A pen!" Mr. Smith congratulated me and told me what a smart girl I was.

He repeated the process and passed me a ruler. Again I eagerly guessed the correct item and was complimented on my expertise. I was so excited to be right. I was feeling very good about myself as he continued to compliment me.

Next, another surprise item was to be displayed. First I heard the crinkle of paper like a wrapper of some kind being opened. Mr. Smith then took my little hand and gently placed it on the object. My small fingers touched it. "What is it?" he asked.

"I don't know," I replied.

"Touch it some more, Michele, and try squeezing it--that might help you to figure it out." Mr. Smith spoke in a panting breath.

Unsure of myself I spoke hesitantly and said, "Is it a hotdog?"

Mr. Smith seemed as though he did not want the game to be over just yet and said, "Are you sure? Maybe you should feel it some more."

I tugged and pulled and stroked it some more then replied, "Yes I am sure, it is a hotdog." Again I was right and was congratulated. I removed my hands from the object, which by now you may have already figured out was his penis.

Mr. Smith gently covered himself up with a towel, took off the blindfold and told me to go in my room to play now.

This game became a regular event day after day. Strangely enough it was always when no one else was home.

I was very young but I was also very intuitive. Something just didn't feel right about this game but I could not figure out why. My tummy would feel sick after playing this game. The feeling kept getting stronger and stronger each day. Like someone was trying to tell me something.

One day I decided to explore this object even further by passing my hands up and down, squeezing hard on it. It seemed to grow bigger and started to get wet at the end. My curiosity got the best of me and I just had to see this object. What kind of hot dog had wet stuff coming out of the end of it? I also thought I wanted to feel the other side to see if it was the same. So I reached forward even further and felt something different this time.

As I scanned my brain for what it might be I had a sinking feeling in my stomach worse than ever before. It was unbearable, as if something was wrong or I had been really bad and my parents were very angry at me. With that kind of feeling I realized that this could not be a hot dog because hot dogs don't have strings attached or something that felt like hair; besides there was no other end of the hot dog to touch. I immediately pulled my hands away and quickly ripped off the blindfold, only to see a shocking thing: Mr. Smith sitting on the bed with his privates exposed. I screamed and said, "This is not a hot dog," and went to run away.

Mr. Smith grabbed my wrist with such strength I could not pull away. His face got really mean, cinched up and red as he leaned towards me and said in a very deep, angry voice, "If you tell anyone about this you will be in trouble. I will make sure you never see your brother and sister again." Yanking my arm towards him and leaning even closer into my face he shouted, "Do you understand me?"

With tears in my eyes and absolutely terrified of this giant man expressing such anger towards me, I promised to never say a word. After a few seconds Mr. Smith released my wrist and I ran crying downstairs to the bathroom and locked myself in until Mrs. Smith got home.

Needless to say the game was never played again after that. Almost every night I would get up out of bed and go downstairs to the bathroom and continuously flush the toilet. Each time Mrs. Smith would get up and say in a soft-spoken voice, "Do you have to go to the bathroom, dear?"

I would reply angrily, "No I just want to see the water come in." Not too long after that we children were moved to a new foster home.

Many years passed before I had a suspicion as to why I was flushing the toilet all the time. Even though I was really too young to fully understand it all, I still felt shame and dirty. By flushing the toilet I felt I could become clean or could flush away the bad feeling in my stomach.

The incident was never spoken about until many years later when I was about eighteen. All the family was visiting our father for Christmas. After a few drinks Fred, our father, mentioned how the Children's Aid was a godsend. And that he did not know what he would have done without them. I couldn't take it anymore and blurted out, "Fuck Children's Aid." Now, I never swore in front of my father before but all the pent-up anger and emotions, with the help of a few drinks to loosen up, just came out.

Everyone went silent and my father glared at me with a look of confusion. "Why would you say that?"

I was not one to hide my feelings and instead let it all out. "I was molested by the foster father when I was four. He used to play blind man's bluff with me and make me feel his dick," I said. Before I could finish my sentence my sister Jenny spoke up and said that he used to lie on her on the bed and French neck with her. She asked his children if their dad kissed them funny, they laughed at her and said she was crazy but she knew something wasn't right.

Neither one of us knew this was going on to the other. "Why didn't you tell me?" Fred said with a sadness and anger in his voice.

Jenny answered, "I was scared."

I responded saying that I really did not understand at that age but knew in my stomach something was wrong.

What a release that was for me, finally knowing I was not alone. That was only a small part in the recovery system though and there were other ramifications that as a result of this early molestation would cause me pain throughout my life.

For now let us continue on from the Children's Aid. There were no significant memories of the second foster home for me. However, the third one wasn't as traumatic as the first but all the same was very unpleasant. I remember being sent to school with holes in my underwear beneath my dress. Of course grade one was the time that the boys started pulling up the girls' dresses and skirts to see what they could find.

This was an embarrassing time for me as I walked each day in fear that I would be next. The people in this foster home were Italian and they had three children of their own. My siblings and I were always treated as second rate. The Russos' children had first priority over all the toys and treats. Mrs. Russo had control of the T.V. so the only escape route for me was to watch and dream that my life could one day be different. That was not an option in this house. Mrs. Russo would watch Flip Wilson, news, and other boring shows that I did not enjoy.

Worst of all my memories goes back to the food. It was strange. There were things I did not like but was forced to eat. One day Mrs. Russo ordered me to clean the green peppers she had steamed. With cuts and scrapes on my hands from playing outside in the bushes my hands would sting from the juice of the peppers. The smell of the peppers cooking in the oven would make me feel sick. At the dinner table I looked at my plate and saw this horrible cooked pepper sitting there and suddenly felt very ill. After all I had endured with cleaning and smelling them I could not imagine eating it. I ate everything surrounding it but outright refused to eat the pepper. Well, that was not what Mrs. Russo wanted to hear. She said, "You better eat all of that or you will be punished." I decided nothing could be worse than eating that thing so I opted to take the consequences. At the same time my brother Mason decided he could not eat his either.

We were both sent to our rooms and told we would have to sit on the hardwood floor for the whole night. Every hour or so my bum would start hurting and become numb. When I tried to lie down Mrs. Russo would pass by and say, "Get up; no lying down." This went on for hours until dark. Mason started chewing on the wood of the windowsill. He soon vomited and was beaten for it. It was a long treacherous night for us.

So as you can see it was not as bad as the first home but still not very pleasant. Feeling isolated and neglected, my only strength to survive was my belief that there must be something better. I was still hoping and yearning for my parents to get back together and save me from emotional turmoil. As each situation occurred I documented it in my brain under the category called "warning signs" or "things to watch out for." It was like mentally taking building blocks and stacking them together one by one. Not realizing it at the time but this process would either help or hinder me with the events that would occur in my future. For now I just forgot about it once it was placed there and continued to daydream about my parents' reunion and how wonderful that day would be. Would I ever get my wish or would it simply remain as a dream? The only one who had the answer to this would be my father, an answer that he soon decided to share with me.

CHAPTER THREE

FREE OR NOT

Finally, after three years of us being in the Children's Aid Society, Fred had saved enough money to get an apartment with two bedrooms and asked the judge if he could take the children home with him. The judge agreed and we were finally free from those brutal foster homes.

The years that followed for me from about age seven to thirteen were pretty good. My father tried his best to instill some good values in a secure home environment. I was happy to have most of my family altogether, although we did move a few more times in a fairly short period. This process did not help me to make close connections with people.

Unfortunately, it wasn't enough to erase all the turmoil that had been boiling inside me for all those years. I still did not feel loved. My father did his best but worked shift work as a police officer so there really wasn't a lot of guidance. My mom was hardly ever in the picture and when she was, she was drunk. She would sometimes take us out for a day visit to the Exhibition or a restaurant and it almost always ended in sheer embarrassment for all of us. So Jenny, at the young age of twelve, became a parent to Mason and I, making sure we were fed, clean, and behaved. If you can imagine what three children would be like pretty much raising themselves then you can also understand we were more like wild animals. Well behaved in front of our father for fear he would beat us, which on occasion he did. That was how it was in those days.

Fred was lonely and felt that his children needed a mother figure in their lives. Along came Mavis, a tall black woman from Alabama with no children of her own. Fred and Mavis dated secretly and fell in love. Soon after that the announcement was made that they would be married. I became resentful of Mavis as I still did not feel loved and what little I got from my father was now going to Mavis.

Mavis, not having children of her own, also felt some resentment and jealousy, especially towards me. I was rebellious and refused to obey Mavis's rules. As time went on everything got worse. My siblings and I tried to speak to our father and let him know that Mavis didn't treat us right when he was not home. But Fred would not listen. He always sided with Mavis. Finally everything came to a head and Mavis and I were screaming at each other. Mavis had long, claw-like nails and came at me to scratch me while I was on the phone. I had had enough and took the phone and cracked Mavis over the head. Mavis was holding her head saying, "oh, oh."

Fred came running in the room and grabbed Mavis. Suddenly she was not hurt and was trying to pull away from him as if trying to get at me.

"What the hell is going on?" Fred said, while both Mavis and

I yelled out our stories. Fred turned to me and said, "Why don't you go live with your mother." I was traumatized. How could my father turn against me like that? How could he say go live with my mother when he knew my mother was unfit, living on welfare in the dumps of Toronto wasted on alcohol and pills every day? It was the same as saying why don't you go live on the street.

Now no one loved me, I felt. Angry, stubborn, and with the will to survive anything, I packed my bags and left home at fourteen years old. My father really didn't mean it; he only said those things in a fit of rage. But it was too late. Nothing he could say at that point could change how I felt. Fred never did apologize anyway, he just kept reading the riot act for me to behave, again reaffirming that I was wrong and bad. And he said it didn't matter anyway because he did not want to be alone. He said Mavis was staying and that was that. At that point I knew my father had chosen his new wife over his children.

I had this uncanny will to survive. Even though all these bad things were happening to me I continued to believe there must be something better out there. I could always take something from a situation and learn from it, constantly adding new strengths to my being. My interpretation of things was not always accurate at the time but with my understanding or belief system somehow it gave me the strength to endure the next phases of my life.

The fact that I was not loved by those around me made me realize I needed to find it elsewhere. My journey began as I arrived at my mother's place with my brother in hand, who was twelve at the time. When everything happened at home with Mavis, Mason decided he did not want to stay there alone and begged to come with me. Jenny had already left home at sixteen after a physical altercation with Mavis months prior to the fight with me. Feeling protective of my brother I decided to bring him along.

It was scary to be alone going to a new location very unfamiliar to us, yet exciting for me to be somewhere new. I was deeply holding on to the thought that my mother had to love me.

We arrived near the address our mom had given us. It looked like a storefront from afar. There were several guys outside, all dark-haired, mostly short but really good-looking. They watched us carefully as we approached. The men began whistling and shouting flirtatious comments like, "Hey Suzie," to me while eyeing me up and down. I immediately responded with, "My name is not Suzie." They laughed and spoke some foreign words that I did not understand at the time. Later I found out it was Portuguese. My brother and I scooted past them and up a long staircase towards our mother's apartment. The hallways were dark and narrow, barely room for two people to walk side by side. Knock, knock, knock on apartment number two. Moments later our mother answered the door. She was quite a large woman, about five feet tall weighing about two hundred and fifty pounds at that time. She had dark curly brown hair, wearing a flowered summer dress.

She hugged both of us strongly telling us how happy she was to see us. She showed us around the apartment first through the dining room, which was where we entered. There were boiler heaters at the back wall with a piece of wood on top with lots of little knickknacks. To the right in another room there was a long narrow kitchen with a fridge, stove, and cupboards. Behind that was the bathroom. A huge ball and claw foot, oval shaped, deep bathtub. I, who loved baths, thought this was amazing. To the left of the tub was a small sink and toilet. Again another long narrow room just like the kitchen. Mason was a little disappointed as there was no shower. He loved showers.

My mother took us back through the kitchen entrance past the dining room to the living room. A small couch was situated against the wall to the left, a coffee table in front with an ashtray, a pack of cigarettes and lighter on top. There were ripped pieces of cigarette packs neatly piled for notes with a pen. On the other side across from the couch was a small black-and-white T.V. and couch chair in front of the closet door; the only closet in the apartment, actually. Through the living room at the back was a bedroom with a single bed and only one dresser. "This is where you will both sleep because I sleep on the couch," my mother said.

Well it was nothing like my father's house, which was about two thousand square feet with four bedrooms, two living rooms, two basements and a walkout to the back yard full of fruit trees and a grape vine. But it didn't matter because my mother loved me and would treat me right and there was no mean stepmother to abuse us.

That night my mother made her famous curry dish, which we really loved. Everything was perfect; I could not ask for anything more. This went on for several weeks and then it was time for me to go to summer camp. It was already paid for and arranged before I left my dad's. I felt bad leaving my brother by himself. I knew my mother would be there and I really wanted to go.

So off I went to Camp Mini-Yo-We in Huntsville. This was a Baptist camp that my siblings and I had attended for several years each summer. It was a place where everyone loved everyone. God became a big part of my life in a time of much sorrow. Even though we were born and raised as Catholics there were no free scholarships that my mother could find, except one for people who attended the Baptist church, so that was where we went. Even though my mother did not have custody of us when we were small she still tried her best to give us something back. Camp was the greatest gift of all.

I loved camp. I would wake up in the morning to a trumpet sound and all the campers and counselors would have to run to the nearest flag pole. It did not matter what you looked like or how you were dressed, you just had to be there. So many people who were not early birds would arrive in their pajamas with their hair sticking up in the air.

Standing quietly, O' Canada would be played over the loudspeaker and everyone would stand tall, very patriotically. Then a prayer was said to thank God for the day and a reading of psalms from the Bible. I believe this was a process of first expressing gratitude for the day ahead but also to make sure everyone was awake. If you weren't awake after all this then you had to be dead. Then it was back to our cabins to get dressed and ready for breakfast at seven a.m.

The standard breakfast was cafeteria style, where the girls would very orderly go one cabin at a time to get their food and bring it to the table. All together we would sing a prayer before anyone could eat. As you can see by now singing was a big part of the day. Singing praises to the Lord of gratitude. After breakfast the first day everyone would meet with their counselors to see what activities they had been assigned for the week. There was swimming lessons, canoeing, camp craft–how to survive in the wilderness--and crafts. Each girl would go to their activities throughout the morning and part of the afternoon following lunch. Of course the same rituals happened at lunch as it did with breakfast with a song and prayer.

Following the early afternoon activity there was a one-hour rest period back at your cabin. No talking aloud at that time. If you wanted to sleep you could. When the hour of quiet time was up it was time for Bible study. The rest of the afternoon was free time where you could go swimming, go down the zip line, make things out of clay or practice your verses from Psalms to memorize. On the last day there was a test to see who could remember it word for word and say it out loud. I loved this part because I had a good memory and always liked to prove I was the best. Also if you could still remember it at the camp reunion that was halfway through the year then you could win a free two-week session at camp.

Early evenings after dinner everyone would gather around a campfire and sing songs created mostly from Bible text. After the first week there would be visitor's day where your parents could come up and visit you to see how things were going. What a great time Camp Mini-Yo-We was for me. I don't know if my life would have turned out the way it did without this experience. Many hard times throughout my life to come I would sing camp songs and cry while praying to God for help. This seemed to calm me in a time of great need.

Meanwhile back in Toronto my mom had started drinking. Mason was becoming lonely and bored and my mom didn't know what to do. She had spent so much time away from her children that these skills were not strengthened, as they would normally have been for someone else. The more

Mason said he was bored and needed something to do, the more she gave him money to go downstairs to the pool hall to play video games. When our father would call Meigan, she would say Mason was out.

Fred became quite worried wondering where Mason so young could be all by himself at night. He could hear in Meigan's voice that she had been drinking and remembered what this was like. Mavis and Fred decided to see for themselves and went down to Toronto. When they got there they knocked on the door. Meigan said "Come in," not knowing who it was and was too wasted to get up anyway. Fred and Mavis entered and saw Meigan lying on the couch with a bottle of vodka three-quarters empty. Cigarette butts filled the ashtray and empty cans of sardines and tuna lay about. There in the corner was young Mason sitting and trembling. He looked like he had not bathed, with greasy blond hair, dirt on his face and his clothes were all wrinkled. Fred immediately took Mason and his things and brought him home.

When I arrived a week later when camp was over I found my brother was missing and my mother was not the same. I barely recognized her lying there. The apartment smelled and the filth and garbage was everywhere. The ashtray was overflowing with cigarette butts. There were empty cans of food, wrappers, and liquor bottles strewn about. My mother could barely talk. Her face was swollen and drool dripped down her cheek like a leaky tap. After a closer look I glared down at my mother and noticed she was lying in her own pee. "Mom, Mom, wake up," I said. "Where is Mason?"

All that came out of Meigan's mouth were sounds. Her eyes were glossy and rolling around. I didn't know what to do. I wouldn't dare call my father, as I knew he would only say I told you so and tell me to get back home. What was worse, I thought, staying here or going back to face my wicked stepmother and all her rules? Out of sheer panic I decided to call the only mother I had ever known, my sister Jenny. Jenny always had all the answers. Very soft hearted and caring. No matter what you did she never stayed angry and always tried to help. I remembered her being the one person who always believed in me no matter what. After several rings Jenny answered the phone. "Hello," I heard.

"Jenny, it's Michele."

"Where are you?" Jenny asked.

"I am at Mom's. I just got back from camp. Mom is sleeping and looks like she has been drinking. She can barely talk and she is lying in her own pee. Mason is gone and I don't know where he is."

Jenny's voice spoke calmly. "Mason is back at Dad's. He came to get him when you were at camp." Some relief was felt by me at that moment knowing my brother was safe.

"What do I do about mom, Jenny?"

"Don't worry," she said. "I will be over there as soon as I can to help." Jenny was so good like that. I spent the rest of my time cleaning up until my sister arrived.

When Jenny arrived she quickly put on a pot of coffee and proceeded to wake our mother up. Between the two of us we managed to wake her, get her cleaned up and get some coffee in her. Meigan was still really out of it but at least she was sitting up and somewhat talking, making some sense. Jenny explained to me that she wished I could stay with her but she was only renting a room from her friend and they wouldn't let anyone else stay there. "Maybe you should go back and live with Dad, Shell?" "Shell" was what my family called me.

"No I can't," I said, "you know how Mavis treated us. I can't bear to go back there." Jenny understood and said to our mother, "You have to stop drinking, Mom, or the Children's Aid will take Michele away." Mom promised she would not drink anymore. Jenny had to leave to go to work so she told me to be careful and to call if I needed anything. "Most of all don't let Mom drink anymore," Jenny warned.

CHAPTER FOUR

FRIEND OR FOE

This next part of my story I have buried so deep within my soul that I am not sure how I will have the strength and willpower to expose it. Feelings of shame and embarrassment create a trembling inside. Still in search of love, having no concept of its meaning to carry me through, resulted in trial and error. This yearning inside to feel appreciated kept calling out. While each day the masculine vultures in heat would prey on me. Comment calling out from the men in front of the pool hall below my mother's place, telling me how beautiful I was and insinuating they could make me feel even more attractive, and a strange friendship soon began.

Let me explain what the final straw was that broke the camel's back, as they say, which resulted in the final day at my father's place before he kicked me out. I had gone down to visit my mother several times with one of my friends. Of course those Portuguese men wanted more from us young girls than they originally made us believe. One in particular, whose name was Joe. A very good-looking guy, with blue-black hair, nice shaped body and a great smile. He always showed special attention to me, acting as if he was now my boyfriend. Meeting me in the back alley behind the pool hall he would hold me tight while kissing me deeply with his tongue. This would happen a lot.

Then one day he took out his penis and had me feel it. Subconsciously I remembered this experience and sort of came to an understanding that this must have been how one shows love. Joe pleaded with me to help him feel even better by going down on my knees and sucking on it. He said that big girls do this kind of thing and it makes their boyfriends happy. I obeyed like a naive girl would.

After it was all over I was so excited that I had done something good that I told my trusted sister Jenny. I vaguely remember my sister giving me a lecture saying you shouldn't do these things. But the feeling of being loved crowded my mind and would not let anything negative in. Again I couldn't hold back on my excitement, searching still for some positive affirmation that what I had done was good so I told my half-sister Jessie.

Jessie had the same mother as me but a different father and was ten years older. Jessie felt she needed to protect me and figured she would tell Mavis and my father so they could get me some help. As the story goes that completely backfired as Mavis started calling me a slut and that was when the fight broke out. And you know the rest.

Believe it or not, I was a good kid. A straight-A student in school, very athletic, attending various running clubs before and after school. I was probably one of the few kids at that time who actually liked doing school work even though I never really fit in socially, always feeling different to the rest. I had few friends growing up. Partially due to the fact that we moved a lot and attended so many new schools. Throughout all of that I had become very insecure. I could not bear any more rejection so I either kept quiet or chose a friend I could protect from all the bad people out there.

Now, I was living with my mother and the time was soon approaching to go back to school. My previous school was way too far away. Not only did I want to attend school to learn more as this was my passion, it was also illegal for a minor up until the age of sixteen not to attend. They would for sure take me away from my mother's place and where else would I go. While my mother was sober one day she called and registered me for the nearest high school.

Excited and nervous I walked over to the new school for my first day. As I approached I saw a massive building surrounded by hundreds of teenagers. My body seized up and my mind kept telling me over and over how I could not possibly bear to go through with this. I remembered being teased in all the new schools and with little self-confidence to back me up my mind was winning.

I took a few more steps closer and suddenly I imagined all the kids outside the school turning and staring at me. I couldn't do it. The power of insecurity was too strong. My body refused to go any further. At that point I made a decision to turn around and go back home. The further away I got the more I regained my strength. Oxygen began to flow throughout and a comforting feeling of normalcy returned.

When I arrived home I began crying, telling my mother that I just couldn't do it. Then I called my sister to hopefully gain her approval or find some alternatives since Jenny always knew what to do. Jenny was understanding and knew about my insecurities and how difficult it must have been for me. She suggested correspondence that you could do from home, self-directed. "That was a great idea," I said.

Jenny then directed me to whom I could call to set this up. CALL!!! I felt a panicked feeling come over me again like when I approached that school. My vision blurred while the blood pumped profusely to my brain. "I can't Jenny, I am too nervous to call." Jenny realized how I was feeling and decided she would make the call for me. "Thank God for Jenny," I thought.

Meanwhile Fred and Mavis were very concerned about me living at my mother's. Soon after they found out that I was not in school they decided I would be better off in the Children's Aid Society and called the police. When they arrived at the door my mom had a bottle of liquor by her side and she had taken a few shots from it already. Technically my mother did not have custody of me. The fact that I was not in school and the booze sitting on the floor was a positive indication to the police that this was not the best place for a fourteen-year-old girl to be.

The police took me to the station and contacted the Children's Aid Society, where a group home was arranged. The Children's Aid worker explained this was different to a foster home as there would be many children there with a mother and father. I was not that happy at my mother's and really wanted to go back to school but was too afraid to go on my own. Maybe this way there would be other new kids and I would have someone else to go with, I thought.

The Children's Aid worker and I arrived at the door of a large two-storey home and were greeted by Mr. and Mrs.

Lester and were taken inside to the kitchen. There were other children looking on and Mr. Lester told them very nicely that they would have lots of time to meet their new guest and they should go do something else.

The Children's Aid worker made some minor introductions to Mr. and Mrs. Lester. She told them that I was having a hard time at home with my father and the law could not allow my mother to take care of me. The Lesters seemed so nice and friendly. I was very excited I would finally have a good home to live in. After the social worker left Mrs. Lester showed me to my room, which I would share with another girl. A grand tour of the house was given and all introductions were made.

Every morning I would get up before school and go jogging at four a.m. I had a little pedometer attached to my waist that would tell me how many miles I had gone. I was clocking four miles a day by that time. I was back in school, excited to do my homework each night, striving for perfection.

I soon realized that none of the other kids had the same desires. I didn't care though because I loved running and being creative with my school work. At night time all the girls would gather round to watch T.V. Everyone would be trying to get to know each other. One loud-mouthed girl named Marcia Morris was specifically interested in me. She must have smelled my innocence. Marcia would be talking about things I knew nothing about or didn't participate in, like drinking alcohol, partying, and smoking.

One day Marcia said a word that I had not heard before. The word was "toke." Feeling like a superstar in school, winning most spelling bees and with knowledge of most words I was curious why I did not know this word. I scanned my brain to see if I could find the meaning, but nothing appeared. Finally I asked Marcia, "What is a toke?"

Everyone started laughing and Marcia said, "You don't know what a toke is?"

I said, "No, and what is so funny?"

"Don't you smoke pot?" Marcia asked.

"No, I don't know what that word is. I don't even smoke cigarettes because it's bad for you," I replied.

Marcia was very streetwise, as they called it back then. She quickly latched on to me hoping to have a partner in crime and introduce me to what she thought were the finer things in life. With so many insecurities I was considered a bit of a follower back then, except for the two things I loved most: school and running. Although I wouldn't do things I knew were wrong, I would follow along and say I liked the same music as them, not really knowing what I liked but just to fit in.

Marcia got closer to me as the days passed, feeding me all kinds of stories like, "We should run away together, I have friend's places we could stay at. You won't have to go to school or put up with any rules." I refused, thinking I loved school and didn't want to get into any trouble.

Meanwhile, the nice Mr. Lester whom I met when I first got there started to show his true colors. He and Mrs. Lester kept questioning me about where I was going at four a.m. I repeatedly told them I was jogging and showed them my pedometer to prove how many miles I went. They didn't believe me and forbade me to leave the house each morning. I was devastated.

At this point I had figured out that I was the only good kid there. I was doing my homework when no one else was. I jogged every morning, keeping healthy, and all the other kids were smokers. All the same feelings erupted from within me, bringing back all the memories of my wicked stepmother. The more Mr. Lester badgered me, the angrier I became. There was always Marcia in the background trying to coax me to run away.

I felt so frustrated one day that I took a pocket knife and carved, "Mrs. Lester sucks bigger dicks than I do," in the wood paneling on the walls of the basement. No one saw me so I figured there were many girls that could be blamed. Mr. Lester was furious. He called all the girls down to the basement. He pointed at the writing on the wall and said, "Who did this?" No one answered. He made everyone sit down on the couch and yelled and screamed about it for an hour, repeatedly asking who did it. When he got to the end of the cigarette he was smoking he said, "I know exactly who did this, you fuckin' bitch," and threw his lit cigarette at me. I was shocked. There was no way he would have known it was me, so I confidently told him I did not do it. Now he was just picking on me again, centering me out.

Although I did not know at the time that in my Children's Aid file were the details of me behind the pool hall with the Portuguese guys. So this was the real reason Mr. Lester thought this was me. Without knowing that and after being banned from jogging in the morning I felt I was being unfairly treated. Needless to say Mr. Lester grounded me to the house indefinitely. I could only leave to go to school and back.

There was Marcia waiting for this moment to go in for the kill. This was her chance to finally convince me to run away with her, while I was at my weakest point feeling like I was fighting a losing battle. There was no more hope for me. No one to love and care for me, everyone was against me making accusations upon me. Maybe Marcia would help me escape from this life. Oh how I wanted to forget all this pain. Marcia did say she had something that would make me feel wonderful. It was time to go on a most interesting journey of my life. I truly believed this would make me feel better.

CHAPTER FIVE

TEEN HITS THE STREETS

Marcia and I packed our bags and waited until no one was around so we could sneak out the door. Off we went as I put all my trust in this worldly teenager. Several bus rides took us to an area called Regent Park. I of course did not know anything about the area until much later. Regent Park was the projects, a community of low-rise apartments packed together providing low-income families a cheaper place to live. Most of the people who lived there were on welfare. For those of you that don't know, this is government assistance. For some reason those on assistance were tough. Maybe because they were poor and had to develop many survival techniques in order to make it through life.

There were so many people in the same situation packed in a small area that most people knew each other. One could not help but learn the techniques of others while living in such close quarters, bad or good. Just to give you an idea of the magnitude of this area, Regent Park was ranked number one at the time for crime statistics in the Toronto area. For me as naive as I was it was like taking a baby and putting it in the middle of a wolves' den. Thank goodness in a way that I had Marcia Morris to guide me along the way. Marcia knew everyone, she was so worldly.

The two of us arrived at an apartment door. Loud music and voices echoed inside. Marcia knocked loud so they could hear and all went silent. Some shuffling and scurrying noises inside and moments later a boy about fourteen answered the door. He immediately recognized Marcia and let us in.

Inside there were many kids throughout the room. Some were sitting and some standing. There in the back sitting on a couch chair was what looked like the only parent there. A large woman with shoulder-length greasy brown hair, wrinkled unmatched clothes, speaking with a deep harsh voice. Marcia whispered some words to the boy who answered the door. As if for approval he walked over to the woman and said something quietly and she gave a slight nod with her head.

The boy then went into a back room and came out with a baggy full of something that looked like tea leaves to me. Marcia exchanged money for the package; thanked the woman and the two of us left the apartment. Marcia took me part way down the stairs and said to stop there. She pulled out the bag and said, "This is what I was telling you about. Pot." Marcia proceeded to pull out a small piece of paper from a package in her pocket and took out some of the pot to roll it inside the paper. When she was finished it looked like a skinny cigarette. She called it a joint and passed it to me.

"I don't know what to do with this," I said.

"Here, I will show you," Marcia said while taking back the joint and puffing on one end while lighting the other. She held her breath for a few seconds afterward before blowing out the smoke. "Here, Michele, you do it now and don't forget to hold it in."

I held the joint to my lips and took a big haul trying to hold it in. But as the smoke hit my throat I began to choke, coughing and coughing. I had never even smoked a cigarette before this. Marcia laughed and said, "Don't worry; it gets easier." After a few more draws I started to get the hang of it. But now something else was happening. I felt dizzy and light-headed and told Marcia this. Again Marcia reassured me that this was good; that I was now high.

We laughed and we laughed. Everything just seemed funny after that. Marcia took me everywhere. We would meet guys while walking around who would always offer us rides or ask us to party with them. The more the merrier, was the saying.

Each night it was a different place to sleep since we did not have a place of our own. Even if we had the money the landlords would not rent to teenagers without their parents' consent. So we partied and we partied forgetting about all our troubles. This was great I thought because I could not remember any of my life's problems. Actually I didn't remember a lot from that time. I was so drugged that only the dramatic incidents were clear in my mind but the in-between situations were quite vague.

I remembered the first night when Marcia could not find a place for us to stay. She had exhausted all her options and she had another idea. "Let's walk down Yonge Street where lots of guys in cars go by and we'll get picked up to go party with them at their house." I followed, thinking this would be a good idea and that we did not have much choice. Marcia neglected to fill me in on the fine details of how this would happen until we arrived at the first house. Sure enough a couple of guys stopped and picked us up and brought us to their house.

After about an hour of partying, smoking dope, and drinking, Marcia leaned over and asked me, "Which one do you want?"

"What do you mean?" I asked curiously.

Marcia proceeded to tell me that, "They won't let us stay here unless we give it up."

I, as innocent as I was, asked, "What does that mean, give it up?"

She said we would have to go to bed with them and have sex. I only thought I had sex before when Joe from the pool hall took me to the park one night. I was wearing a skirt and Joe laid on top of me, kissing me and feeling me. It was almost like a dream for me. The way he made my body feel sort of put me in a daze. When Joe got up off me I realized he had pulled my panties down part way and I was all wet. I gathered myself together, pulled up my panties and went home.

All I knew then about sex was that when a guy breaks your virginity you bleed. So I quickly ran to the washroom to check it out; nothing, just wet. I knew I didn't pee myself; it would have been even more wet, and it would smell like pee and it didn't. After speaking to all my friends after that they all agreed that I had sex. The reason for not bleeding was probably because I used to do gymnastics, they said. They had heard that sometimes this causes the hole to break open early. So I figured this must have been sex. I had imagined there would have been more to it, some big spectacular event, but it wasn't. No big deal.

When Marcia mentioned that we would each need to have sex with one of the guys in order to have a warm place to sleep for the night I figured it was no big deal, based on my previous knowledge. There was where it began. The higher I got the easier it became. Even the ugly guys were good looking when you were stoned.

Every night was a different guy or guys. Sometimes more than one as all of them who were there expected to be satisfied. I felt I was becoming an expert at this. I learned all different techniques: up, down, around and placing it in all the holes that it could fit.

For some reason I just couldn't get enough. What I did not realize at the time was that while the men were getting satisfaction having an orgasm, I myself was not. I didn't even know what this was. All I knew was I wanted more. Still, feeling like this was the closest thing to love that I could get and did not want it to stop.

Every night a different guy and a different story which seemed to work well as long as you said yes. But what if we did not want to have sex what would happen?

Well one night Marcia and I just planned to party with this group of guys and then go and find where Marcia's sister lived to stay there. After a few drinks we decided to leave. These guys just didn't seem nice, hollering out rude sexual comments. On our way out the guys decided they wanted sex and they were going to get it. Both Marcia and I repeatedly said, "No, leave us alone." Marcia was dragged into one room and me into another. They held me down and ripped my clothes off and proceeded to have violent intercourse with me one after another as I screamed and cried for them to stop. They had ripped my insides and all I could feel was pain. The one guy decided to spray shaving cream on my vagina. "Ouch," I screamed and cried saying "No, it's burning, help." I was so loud they were afraid the neighbors would hear.

All I kept thinking about as I ran out of the door was that I had been raped and violated. How horrible and shameful it felt. I knew the police were looking for me because I was considered a runaway and underage to be on my own. I could not call them. What about my Dad, I thought. After all these months of me not being around surely he would be grateful to hear from me. He would protect me and be angry that these men would violate his daughter so. I found a phone booth and reached in my pocket for some change to make the call. It was three a.m. and my father answered the phone. As the tears poured down my cheeks I cried out for help. "Dad, please help me. I was raped by a group of guys."

His reply was something that would sit with me for many years to come. "Don't call here anymore; I do not want to talk to you."

I was devastated. My mouth hung open in shock as my father hung up the phone. Feeling completely abandoned without as much as my own father to care for me. I knew now in my heart that he really didn't love me. I suspected it when he basically forced me out me out and chose my stepmother over me but I didn't really believe it until now.

Sirens sounding in the background quickly snapped me out of my state. I realized they would be looking for me and ran.

Not fast enough because they caught me and threw me in the cruiser. I had no idea what happened to Marcia and couldn't even remember which house we were in. I was so high when I went in and ran so quickly afterward, relieved to have gotten away, that I did not think to look. Needless to say when I explained to the police that I had been raped but could not describe where I was they did not believe me. As soon as they found out I was a runaway they hauled me in to the station.

I always felt comfortable with the police because of my Dad I suppose, and growing up around them. I was bright and not yet tarnished. They could see my innocence beneath my tough exterior. I had not committed any criminal acts, I was just a runaway so I posed no threat to the police. I was polite and talkative to the officers. Smiling most of the time, I think they felt for me. They knew somehow that I was not too far gone and maybe could be helped. So they were nice to me. I had heard horror stories from some of the people that I partied with of the things cops would do to people. I never did understand how that could be. Especially now when I was being arrested and they were all nice to me.

When the police asked, "Where do you live?" I replied, "Nowhere; on the streets sometimes."

"What about your parents?" they asked.

"My mother is an unfit alcoholic and my father doesn't want me. He chose my stepmother instead." The officer's only choice was to call the Children's Aid Society (C.A.S.) since the original missing persons report was from the group home that we ran away from anyway. The C.A.S. arrived only a couple of hours later.

Everything was different now. I had many new experiences

to add to my belt. First and foremost I had a taste of freedom. No one to boss me around, no rules to adhere to. Yes in the C.A.S there would always be food and a warm bed to sleep in that was true. But no drugs or alcohol to help forget about the pain of being unloved and that meant more to me.

I had made my decision. I would go to the foster home willingly and let all involved think I was going to listen and stay. Then at first opportunity when no one was looking I would slip away and try to find Marcia. I could always crash at my mother's the odd night if I had to.

When I entered the foster home I felt a sunken feeling in my stomach. It just didn't feel right to be there. If I had any doubts before of whether this was the right thing to do or not, I did not have any now.

Before morning hit I gathered my things and listened to hear if everyone was sleeping. I slowly made my way to the front door, tiptoeing all the way. Holding on to my shoes I unlocked the door quietly and eased my way out without anyone hearing me, put my shoes on and made my way down the road to a bus top. Best thing to do for me would be to make my way to my mother's and make some calls from there. Maybe get some money.

When I arrived my mother was glad to see me and offered me a drink and a cigarette. I didn't smoke at this point nor did I feel like drinking. I knew the police would probably come there to see if I was there so I could not stay long. I was able to get in touch with Marcia and would soon meet her on the other side of town.

Marica and I met up and after a few hours discussing the previous evening's events we made our way out to party some more. A few more weeks of the same life continued with sex, drugs, partying, and finding a place to stay each night. Marcia finally got the address of one of her sisters. She knew she would let us stay there. So off we went to an apartment downtown.

There were a few people sitting around when we got there. When Marcia asked where her sister was they said, "in the back room; she will be right out." While we were waiting a couple of the guys started rolling a joint. Everywhere we went there was this ritual going on, a process of pulling out rolling papers with their head hanging down bent over a coffee table, a bag of weed sitting on the side that they would dip their fingers in to pull out a few sprigots, breaking them into small bits and placing it in the paper, rolling it up and sharing it out with the rest. So we could all get high together.

This was the first time I heard the song "In the Flesh" by Pink Floyd. It completely freaked me out, especially being in a strange place. I could hear sounds of babies crying in the background. I was so high from the marijuana that I didn't realize it was coming from the music.

I looked around frantically for the baby and at the others in the room to see if they were concerned. No one seemed to be fazed by this and I couldn't understand that. "Did you hear that?" I said. Everyone laughed. 'How can they be so inconsiderate,' I thought and got up and went to go towards the washroom hoping I would be able to see this child in need. I could hear smacking or slapping noises on skin and lots of swearing going on as if someone was angry. The sounds got louder as I approached the door next to the bathroom. The door was slightly open just enough for me to see a large woman with a belt tied around her arms and ankles and a man standing around pacing with a syringe in his hand.

I quickly ran back into the living room and relayed this info to Marcia. She said, "Ya my sister is shooting up and probably can't find any more veins to work with."

"What!" I said in shock. "What do you mean?"

"She is shooting drugs in her veins, probably heroin, she is ok," Marcia said nonchalantly. "Maybe we should go, Michele, because she will be pretty out of it when she comes out," Marcia suggested. I couldn't get out of there fast enough. I was completely scared of this unknowing world I had embarked on.

Marcia and I spent the next few weeks roaming around staying at different places. We met some people who told us there was an apartment building where the landlord was in jail and the guy in charge had a key to all the units and he would let people stay in one of the apartments for free. Well, this seemed perfect so we ventured down to an area called Parkdale. Now Parkdale was second on the list of dangerous crime areas at that time.

Marcia felt it was time to introduce me to another drug called acid. She gave me a tiny piece of paper and told me to put it on my tongue for a minute and swallow it. Marcia told me how much I would love it and how it would make me feel. It only took about twenty minutes before I started feeling the effects, right around the time we arrived at the building where we might be able to get an apartment. Marcia did all the talking to a long-haired dirty-looking guy who came to the door. He said that he had a few places left and showed us to ours.

It was a bachelor apartment with kitchen, bath, and bedroom all in one room. We were thrilled since this would be way better than sleeping at strangers' places or on the streets as we had in the past. After the last incident I did not want to go that route. The long-haired guy said "Once you're settled you girls come on over to my unit for a beer." My head was starting to spin from the acid. It felt as though the room was moving around. I told Marcia this and as always Marcia assured me this was part of the high. We put away our duffle bags in the room, which was all we could carry. It had all the essentials, a few changes of clothes, toothbrush, toothpaste, and hair and makeup supplies enough to last us about a week. It seemed for me that I was moving in slow motion. Every move I took seemed to take twice as long as normal.

Off we went down the hall to Jeff's place, the long-haired guy. When we arrived there were a few guys sitting around and Jeff was rolling a joint. There was some small talk going on. Jeff was from Newfoundland and had a very strong accent. The more I got higher from the acid and then smoking the pot the harder it was for me to understand Jeff. Then the giggles came. The more he talked the more he sounded like he was mumbling, the whole time with a completely serious face. He had a missing front tooth and the rest were yellow and rotten. His face looked like it was changing colors. While Marcia and I kept laughing I started pointing at Jeff's face, saying it is changing colors. "Look, it's red, now blue, can you see that," I said. Jeff was insulted and we couldn't stop laughing. The tears were rolling down our faces.

The two of us realized we were out of control and apologized, telling Jeff that it was because we were stoned on acid. He was a pretty forgiving dude but we still knew we should get out and go for a walk. I don't remember where Marcia went after that. I found myself lying on the front porch watching the horses run by and the waterfalls go down the curb. Of course this was completely a hallucination as this could not be happening in the middle of the city. I lost track of time but it all seemed to last forever.

Finally, after hours of heart-racing visual effects I came down off the high. In some respects I liked to be in control and this drug did not allow for that. One thing it did do just like the rest was it helped me forget that I really was all alone out there without my family.

We partied by day wherever we could. Marcia would buy large quantities of pot and my mother would give me pills she got from her doctor. We would use some of the drugs and sell the rest for food and drink money while each evening having a room to safely sleep in. This worked out great for a couple of weeks. Then one day Jeff went running through the halls in a panic saying the guy who owns this place is getting out of jail today and everyone has to leave. Our dream location was over. We quickly stuffed our things in our duffle bags and off we went back to the streets.

It was winter now, very cold outside and lots of snow. We couldn't possibly sleep on the street or in an ally way like we had done previously when there was nowhere else to go. Marcia had an idea. She called her sister and she said we were welcome to stay there. Marcia said her sister had straightened herself out from the last time we were there so it would be ok.

That night it was freezing outside, about minus twenty, and there was snow everywhere. Marcia and I arrived at her sister's apartment and rang the buzzer. No one answered. We kept ringing it repeatedly, shaking frantically from the cold, but still no answer. Marcia said maybe her sister was out. She was sure she would be back soon. She suggested we go somewhere warm while we waited for her to come home.

As we got to the end of the walkway we saw a stretch limousine parked in front. There was a door opened and there was a fat older man and a thin tall young woman inside. The man called out, "Are you looking for someone?"

Marcia answered, "Yes, my sister; she lives right there."

He asked what her name was and she said, "Sheila." He said "We are waiting for her too. Why don't you sit inside this warm car while you wait?" Wow, perfect timing I thought because I wasn't sure if I could take much more of the cold. Both of us climbed in the car.

After waiting about a half hour the man said "Well it looks like she is not coming home tonight. I have a spare room at my apartment if you would like to stay there for the night." We quickly looked at each other and agreed this would be best. On Spencer Avenue in Parkdale, a high-rise building about twenty stories high is where we ended up that night. We didn't know it yet but we were headed for even more trouble than we had experienced so far.

The door was opened and all four of us entered. What a strange place, I thought. There was a kitchen, small dining room, living room and two bedrooms. What was strange about it was that it was practically empty. Not much furniture or knickknacks, no pictures on the wall. Just one couch, a coffee table, and two bedrooms with a bed in each and one included a low long dresser with mirror on top.

The man sat on the couch and pulled a baggy out of his pocket and a razor blade and set it on the table. "Sit down girls, relax," he said. Obediently we did as he said, curious about the bag of beige powder he laid on the table. He poured some out and began to spread it around with the razor into long strips. Marcia asked what it was and was told it was speed. We had heard this was a good drug through our travels but never had a chance to try it. We were hoping he would offer us some.

He took out a 50-dollar bill and began to roll it into a tube. He then put it to his nose and sucked up the powder until the strip of powder disappeared. The fifty-dollar roll was then passed to the girl he had with him and she repeated the same steps. "How about you girls," he said, "do you want some?" Eagerly Marcia and I both tried snorting this stuff he called speed.

Although I didn't know at the time I did figure out years later after many drug experiences that this could not have been speed. It must have been angel dust, a drug which would create a massive sexual parade of events that evening. The girl that the fat man was with went into one of the rooms and went to bed. The fat old man took Marcia and me by the hands and took us into the other room. Every sexual act occurred that night that you could think of with the three of us. It seemed this drug left us dazed and confused with no strength to back out. When it was all over the fat man did the same with the girl in the other room. But before doing that he had talked to Marcia saying, "You girls can work for me now. I am going in the next room and you are not to leave," he said, as he pulled out a gun and placed it on the dresser in the other room.

I was terrified. I knew guns were not good. Marcia was still quite wasted and thought this was all ok. I told her "We have got to get out of here, do you know what you said to him Marcia? You said we would work for him. He must be a pimp. How will we get out of here?" I said with a panicked voice. Then I thought there must be a way. You see this was always my way of thinking in a bad situation. There was always hope, belief there must be something better. Eventually he would fall asleep and we could sneak out I thought. Hours later that did happen and slowly and quietly we snuck out and ran as far as we could knowing we could never go back to that area again. We would always have to watch our backs for his vehicle nearby.

That was too close for comfort, we could have been beaten, raped, forced to become prostitutes or, even worse, killed. Where would we go now? The only place left was my mother's. I knew the police would look for me there but maybe I thought they had already gone there and realized that I wasn't there and wouldn't check again.

My hopeful attitude would not save me this time. Marcia had an ounce of pot in her purse. We were standing in the hallway at my mother's place when we heard the heavy boots coming up the stairs. "The cops," Marcia said. "We gotta run."

The only way out was an emergency exit at the other end of the hall. But before we tried that Marcia took the pot out of her purse and said, "Here you hold this, I am sixteen, if I get caught they will put me in jail. You are underage so nothing will happen to you."

Again I, not knowing the ramifications of this, believed Marcia and put the pot in my purse. The two of us ran down the hall to the fire escape. By the time we reached the bottom the police were there to stop us. We were taken to the station but only I was charged of course because I was in possession of the drugs.

My world just became way more complicated. At the same time the trust I had placed in my only friend Marcia was shattered. I realized that Marcia had lied to me. It was far too late for regrets. I had dug my hole deeper and now the police could finally try to get me help. All they could do up to now when they found me was place me in a foster home because I hadn't done anything wrong. Now everything would change.

CHAPTER SIX

BEHIND BARS - IS IT REALLY FOR THE BETTER

I was convicted and would be sentenced to nine months in reform school, called training school at the time. Basically it was a jail for juvenile delinquents. I was terrified, how could I survive this? I knew my strength and wisdom came from Marcia but she would not be there to help me through it. There would be lots of really bad kids there who committed murders and armed robberies. I had seen movies that showed these people and how vicious they could be.

Even though I had experienced some pretty bad things over the past few months I really wasn't a bad kid. During the long van ride up to Bowmanville, where the training school was, my heart raced, my neck tightened and my mouth became dry in reaction to my nervousness. All kinds of thoughts ran through my mind as the tears poured down my face. I begged the driver to stop and take me back to the city. I explained that I was not like the others and that they would be mean to me. Maybe beat or even worse, kill me.

None of my efforts seemed to alter the driver's decision. His job was to transport me to the training school and that's what he was going to do. I prayed and prayed for God to help me through this. Suddenly as I arrived strength came over me. It was a false front but I knew it would be necessary for me not to show my weaknesses.

I remembered the guys I had met in the abandoned house and how they taught me to fight with my fists to protect myself if I ever needed it. I also remembered Marcia saying that if you look and act tough people won't touch you because they are afraid you might hurt them.

The driver took me into the office of the Bowmanville Training School to meet the staff. After some initial paperwork a woman took me over to a place they called the store to get new clothes. Wow, I thought this was pretty cool, especially when I saw they had clothes there that were just like I wore on the street. Jeans, t-shirts, running shoes. They even had lumber jackets. I always wanted one of those but couldn't afford it.

It was now time to go into the wolves' den of girls troubled with many issues. I knew from what I had heard so far from my street friends that remaining strong and tough in the midst of these criminals would be the only way I would survive. I needed to let them know that they couldn't push me around. Just before entering the building I made my decision that I would play tough. I took a long deep breath and took a step forward through the door. As I entered I could see a stream of teenagers gathered, staring at this new person who had arrived.

There was a partially enclosed glass separating an office in the center by the entry door with a few desks and filing cabinets and a phone for the staff. To the left behind that was the showers. No shower doors and concrete floors all out in the open. To the right of the office was a large living or sitting room with chairs along the back walls and several big couches, a coffee table and T.V. Around the back wall to the right of the entry door were a few rooms with bunk beds in them. On the other side of the office behind the living room was a large games room with extra beds along the wall. Behind that was a large kitchen with not much in it.

Everyone was checking me out, eyeing me up and down trying to figure out what kind of person I was. After the grand tour the staff showed me to my room and to a bottom bunk. There were about six bunk beds in the same room. This is where I met Nikki.   She followed me in and introduced herself. I was relieved that someone would talk to me. I found out that Nikki was also new and had arrived the day before. No one had accepted her or been very nice so far. I really liked Nikki. I could sense right away that she was a nice girl and we became friends.

While I was on the streets I had sort of taken up smoking. I didn't inhale it and tried to hide this fact but knew it was something people did to look cool. This training school allowed the kids to smoke in designated areas. Strange when you think about how things are now in the world. Even adults aren't allowed to smoke inside places. But that was the way it was back then. They probably figured it would keep everyone calmer, preventing them from going through withdrawals.

Nikki offered me a smoke but I said, "It's ok, I have my own." You weren't allowed to smoke in the bedrooms so Nikki and I went into the living room. Everyone was hanging out there either smoking or watching T.V. No one else introduced themselves to me; they just kept staring and looking over intermittently at this big fat blond girl sitting along the edge of the room. It was as if they were looking for her approval. They were all hovering around her getting her whatever she wanted. I soon figured out this must be the ringleader. She had a deep, hard-sounding voice and she would boss people around. "Get me this and get me that," she would say. It was disgusting, actually, watching people sucking up to her like that. All I could remember hearing was my male friends telling me in my head "Don't let anyone push you around. You have to stand up for yourself or they will always be bothering you."

I decided I would not be doing what these followers did no matter what. After my smoke I went to have a quick washroom break. On my way back into the room the blond fat girl yelled out "Get me a glass of water" and glared at me.

The room went silent, as all eyes and ears rose to attention to see how I would react. Would I run and get the water like everyone else or would I stand up to her. Secretly many of the girls were hoping I would stand up to her as they were tired of being bossed around. They were all so terrified of Cathy, which was her name, but they would not say that out loud. Without giving it any thought and with pure instinct and attitude I shouted loudly with a strong voice, "Fuck You! Get your own water."

Everyone froze in the room as if they all stopped breathing as we both stared each other down with evil intent in our eyes. Nothing more was said that day but the original group that surrounded Cathy began to dissipate and congregate around me. These were the people who were afraid of

Cathy but were tired of being bossed around who came to my side. The ones who stayed were far too terrified of Cathy so they remained with her.

This is where the rivalry began. Cathy's gang versus my gang, and everything became a competition after that, with each side fighting for leadership. Nothing physical had occurred yet; only verbal since everyone knew the rules. If you fought you would get locked up in the diggers. The diggers were a row of holding cells with a small barred window and a metal bed frame with a mattress only at night. Lockup was for twenty-three-and-a-half hours a day and you would be taken for a walk outside for the other half hour. No one wanted to go to the diggers.

As time went on the adrenalin was pumping, emotions were high. The staff could sense the animosity within the group and were watching carefully. Someone in Cathy's group would be rude to a member of my group then retaliation was in order; back and forth this would continue.

My group made some popcorn one night for everyone including Cathy's group. Before you think "Oh how nice," you need to know what was in it. Covered in nice hot butter and a disgusting combination of hork, the popcorn was presented to our nemesis. Yes, everyone spit in it before delivering it to them in the dark T.V. room. They chowed down the popcorn as my group watched with smirks on their faces. No one said anything but inside they knew we won the battle.

More incidents occurred and my team got even more vicious this time, substituting pee for water in a batch of cookie mix. We made one batch with pee for Cathy's group and the staff, and a separate one without it for ourselves. Again secretly chuckling as we watched them eat it and say "These cookies are really good, they are so chewy." Yes, paybacks are a bitch.

Finally everything came to a head. A girl on Cathy's team started arguing with one of my girls. Cathy jumped in and threw her verbal attacks in. I spoke my part, protecting my teammate, telling them to leave her alone. Cathy quickly turned in anger and said, "You stay out of this."

I said, "Fuck you Cathy, you got a problem with that, let's go then, you and me Cathy, right now," edging her on to fight. Cathy backed down and said, "I don't want to fight with you, Michele."

The situation got too close for comfort for the staff. It was almost an all-out gang war. So they decided to lock Cathy up in the diggers. No one could figure out why they only locked up Cathy other than that everyone had heard that Cathy had killed someone before and that was why she was in training school in the first place. Who knows, it could have been a story however, they did keep Cathy in the diggers.

Cathy never returned from the diggers; she was kept in permanent lockup. Because of this the staff felt guilty and offered her to have a visit a day with one of her friends from the house. Shockingly, Cathy chose me. After all we had gone through as rivals, Cathy appreciated that I was the only one willing to stand up to her. Oddly enough Cathy and I became good friends. The rest of the girls in the house were miffed. I was taken out of my programs to talk to Cathy, sometimes being called upon to calm her down when she would freak out.

Two and a half months into my sentence an announcement was made that the Bowmanville Training School would be closed down in a few weeks. All the girls would be sent to the neighboring school in Cobourg. No one liked that because we heard that you can't smoke there and you are locked up most of the time. Whereas at Bowmanville it was a big field and the girls walked to a school on the other side. There was a lot more freedom and the staff were pretty cool, considering. It seemed like they really cared. They were even taking us on a camping and canoeing trip to the French River the following week.

Well there wasn't much I could do about it, I thought at the time. However, this didn't stop me from thinking about possible options on how I could get away before then. I had seen people try to escape from Bowmanville unsuccessfully before. It was surrounded by miles of farmland with no access to the city for miles. As soon as the staff would be alerted to their disappearance, like a swat team they would go out on a search of the surrounding grounds. Eventually they all got caught, even the fastest runners. So leaving from there was not an option.

A week had passed and the girls and staff were loading up a school bus with necessary camping gear to go off into the woods. It didn't seem like that long of a drive to me, most likely because everyone was so excited to get off the property and feel like real people instead of prisoners, so the time passed quickly.

We arrived at a place called "Pine Cove" located right on a lake near the French River. This is where we would start our canoe journey to a deserted island. It was pretty basic camping stuff, a tent, bonfire, swimming, roasting dogs and marshmallows. As exciting as it was to be away from the training school I could not stop thinking about what was to come. The inevitability of being transported to Cobourg where there would be complete lockup and a lot of rules to bear. I racked my brain for ideas and finally a plan came to mind.

I asked the staff if myself and two other girls could go for a canoe ride. Realizing we were way out in no man's land the staff agreed and said don't go too far because dinner will be ready shortly. All dressed in bathing suits and life jackets we girls headed out in the boat. As soon as we got out of sound range of the island I announced my plan. "We could canoe over to that other piece of land over there and get out of the boat, tip it over so they will think we drowned. Then we could make our way through the bush to Pine Cove where our bus was." I continued to say, "We could hot wire the bus and escape. That way we won't have to go to the new training school."

I was a leader type and the two girls in the boat were followers. I convinced them my plan was foolproof and they all agreed. We quickly paddled as fast as we could until we reached land. We tipped over the canoe removed the life jackets and threw them in the water. We began running through the woods for about what seemed like an eternity but was probably only about a half hour or so. There were back flies and mosquitoes biting us constantly. With all of us dressed in skimpy bathing suits and no land in sight this was treacherous.

We began to panic and doubt our decision to escape. I had to come up with another plan to calm them down. I looked around frantically for a way out. There in the distance I saw a man in a boat fishing off to the side of the land we were on. "Quick, let's go ask him if he can drive us to Pine Cove," I announced confidently. Off we went and within minutes arrived at his location.

All of us put on our best theatrical performances telling the man that our canoe tipped and we were stranded and needed to get to Pine Cove. We told him we had been walking for hours and we still hadn't got there. The man said that this was an island and we wouldn't be able to get there on foot. He immediately offered to take us with his boat.

When we arrived at Pine Cove we were relieved to see our bus still parked where we left it. We opened the door and went inside to open the hood. Of course none of us three girls really knew how to hot wire it so after a few tries we decided to grab what we could from the bus, some energy bars and stuff, and abandon the idea. Now we would try to walk and hitch hike along the road.

As we were leaving the bus a young man appeared asking what we were doing. "This is our bus," we said, "we are just getting some things from it."

He pulled out a pocket knife and said, "I don't think you are supposed to be here."

All of us girls in fear quickly said, "it's ok you can have our bus," and headed for the road. We walked along this desolate road surrounded by forest for about a half hour, yet to see a car go by. Then in the distance we saw a car coming. The closer it got the more we could see it was a police car. I directed the girls to act cool like you're just going for a walk. The officer pulled up beside us, opened his window and said, "Hello girls." We responded politely with the same. He then said, "You are the runaways I heard about."

"Runaways, what's that?" The girls replied with astonishment.

The officer put his car in park and said, "Come now, girls, get in the car," and started to open his door. Using a loud voice I shouted, "RUN" and the girls took off into the woods like bats out of hell.

About twenty minutes later we started to venture closer to the road thinking it might be safe to go now and then hopefully we could get a ride from there. We approached the ditch at the side of the road with very high weeds and heard some sounds coming from above. We quickly ducked down. The police were nearby and we heard their walkie-talkies saying that they hadn't seen us yet.

Now, I had an absolute enormous fear of bees. I had run on the road in front of moving cars screaming to get away from them before. While this was all happening the girls and I realized we were surrounded by wasps hanging around in the bush.

They were buzzing and buzzing in our ears, around our faces and necks. One of the girls said, "I don't think I can take it." Her statement brought forth my fears in the forefront of my mind and I realized that I couldn't take it either and gave the ok to go. Of course the police above heard this and gave chase. In through the forest we went jumping logs and dodging trees. I was the fastest and was in the lead looking back over my shoulder each chance I had to check on my girls.

I could only see one behind me and thought the other one might have been caught. Then all of a sudden I heard a loud bang and cracking noise. I stopped and looked back to see one of the girls down yelling, "I think I broke my knee. I can't move." No sooner did she say that, there was an officer at her side. These cops were like giants, about six-foot-four inches and strong country O.P.P. I was the last one, and I knew I could get away because I was fast and agile and would be able to deke them out, even if they got close. I decided to go for it I had gone this far why not.

Everything was fine until a quick-minded officer announced he was giving up and not coming after me. He said, "Good luck to you." He reminded me it would be dark soon and I would be all by myself and there were bears out there. I stopped in my tracks and thought for a moment. Bears! By myself! In the woods! No I don't think so. I turned around and gave myself up. The officers brought us to the O.P.P. station to see what to do. It took several hours for the training school staff to pack up and head on over to the station.

Meanwhile we were having a great time at the station. I had always liked the police. I guess because my father was one and I had grown up around them. I knew if you talked nice to them they would give the same in return. We sat in their chairs with our feet up on the table wearing their police hats charming them up. They brought in burgers for us while we waited. Of course, they gave as many lectures and advice as they could to try to turn us around. That was their job. They said, "You have two options to consider. We can either put you in jail or you could go back with the staff to the training school." Once the staff arrived we had made our decision to go back, as jail was not an option.

On the way home in the bus the staff gave their lectures as well. They also mentioned how stupid it was for us to take off because they were planning on letting us leave up until that point. They said there wasn't enough room for everyone to go to Cobourg so they were given the option to choose some kids to finish their sentence early. That really sucked because if we only knew we would not have done what we did. Too late now, we were off to Cobourg for nine months. Not before a stint in the diggers, though.

Ah the diggers, what really was the theory behind this? My only guess was it was their way of saying, you were bad. So let's lock you up in a four-by-two-foot cell, take out all the comforts of home, leaving you with a metal bed and concrete floor. It is possible they thought this isolation time would give these children time to think about what they did and maybe reconsider duplicating it in the future. I truly believe this theory backfired. Where was the counseling, the guidance, and the caring people to help you find your way? Didn't anybody wonder why these girls were running away in the first place? Asking them in a quick session and demanding a response would only invoke the regurgitation of their cover-up story. There was a reason why these children were astray in their lives, a hidden meaning. This may probably have been the biggest mistake in the history of juvenile delinquent care. You wouldn't tell a stranger your deepest darkest secrets before they have earned your trust. Then why would this be any different? Punishing children only suppresses their inner fears and pains, disabling them from reaching their full potential. Why doesn't everyone see that?

I am not just talking about institutional caregivers; I am talking about everyone in general. Starting from your parents, filtering through to the teachers and coaches and finally to your boss when you start working. It's a vicious circle. In the end all anyone wants is to feel good and to be loved. Ultimately, a result accomplished from being valued and appreciated. To their credit, Bowmanville did go a step further than all the rest, for the most part, treating the children like they were special. They had great teachers at the school programs who tried to connect with each person, initiating interesting assignments which involved their own personal creativity.

For example, English class, where the students were asked to go out and make their own video. And science class where they were allowed to make soapstone pipes. The unfortunate part was these teachers were only in our lives for a short time in the day. But this was the way to gain our trust, get into our minds and help us understand why our lives had gone this way and in the end teach us the coping mechanisms for dealing with adversity. In other words, give us the self-confidence and resources to lead our lives in the right path.

Instead the government cuts the funding for this type of facility, which has the basis of what's necessary and only needs some guidance and direction to complete the task. We can't totally blame the government either. We can only blame ourselves, since the government consists of real people just like you and me. How do you change millions of people? You don't; you just change yourself and everyone will follow. You may only change the life of one person and that person will be the cause of changing the life of another, creating a ripple effect instead of a vicious circle.

Take me for example: you have heard some of my story so far. I felt unwanted from birth and again when my younger brother was born. That feeling later progressed to a feeling of not being loved, especially by the key important people in my life – my mother and father, stepmother, etc.

The next phase was abandonment when my father basically

forced me out and refused to speak with me. These are real feelings whether or not you believe they are justified I still felt them. Bottom line is I did. Yes, I chose the wrong way to deal with them, turning to drugs and sex. What other choices did I have? Who was helping me, guiding me in my time of need? Everyone played their part in my vicious circle including myself.

Other than my strong, independent nature I had an internal belief system that there had to be more, something better. I believed this deeply in my heart and soul. There were a few key people who helped me hold on to this thought, where many others just gave up and let the world cave in around me.

To start with, my sister Jenny, who took care of me throughout my childhood, out of sheer necessity. She made sure I was fed and attending school while my father worked shift work trying to make a life for his children the only way he knew how. Even to the point of being my sole guardian for two whole weeks at the age of twelve when my father travelled to England to visit his family. Jenny was in charge.

So when I had to leave my father and stepmother's home it was Jenny and her understanding voice that I remembered so well. Jenny always without a doubt believed in me. She knew in her heart that I was a good person inside and one day would be successful in whatever I did. When everyone including my father said, "Michele will never make anything of herself, she is just too messed up," Jenny always stepped up to the plate to defend me and give reassurance that things would change. I never forgot this. I didn't realize it at the time how important my sister's confidence in me would mean to my life. It was Jenny's confidence as a child that would give me some type of security in a turbulent world that surrounded me.

Not enough good could ever be said about Jenny. Just think of "Mother Teresa" and the life she lived. The most incredible sacrifices she made to help those in need who were suffering. This is the closest comparison I can give you of Jenny. Ironically enough Jenny's middle name is Teresa. I cannot even express these words to Jenny or even on paper without a fountain of tears and emotions flowing through me.

Then there is Magoo, a selfless Baptist woman from Camp Mini-Yo-We who took it upon herself in light of God's work to reach out to me while I was in training school. She visited me and prayed for me to be saved. I lashed out with mean comments, embarrassed in front of my peers to have such a straight and narrow person come to see me. Magoo gave me reassurance that God loved me anyway and would be there for me whenever I needed him. Although Magoo probably doesn't know this but her presence and words that day gave me another kind of strength to help carry me through the years to come. There would be many desperate situations where I might not have made it out alive if it weren't for the faith I carried with me.

On the verge of suicide in my deepest darkest moments I would suddenly remember the words to the Christian songs from camp. I would chant them over and over again while the tears poured down my face, begging for help out of my desperate situation. God always answers my prayers. Without Camp Mini-Yo-We and Magoo I would not have believed this to be possible.

There were others that I will speak about later when they come into play in my life story.

***

Cobourg training school, now this was much different from Bowmanville. Way more rules and restrictions to start with, and a far less caring staff as you will soon find out.

First you had to be strip-searched before entering. What a humiliating process for a young girl to have to endure knowing full well that these areas are to be kept private. Then for the first month, maybe longer, based on behavior, you had to go into a building which was twenty-three-and-a-half hour lockup. Just like in a penitentiary for hardened criminals, you had to earn the right to leave that building. A group of staff would take the girls out to play soccer and things like that to get fresh air. There was absolutely no smoking allowed. So not only did these girls have to deal with their own personal issues they had to deal with withdrawal at the same time. Not a nice setup.

After a month I was moved to a more open concept where I could go to school and walk there, guarded by staff of course, also for outdoor activities and the mess hall for meals. You would also be allowed to have visitors come up on Saturdays. Jenny would visit whenever she could.

It was a real treat when my mother would visit because she would bring vodka and orange juice in a container and I would share it around to the girls in the waiting room saying out loud, "Would you like some orange juice? Just for the kids; no parents." No one would say anything as they were thrilled for the treat. My mom would also bring cigarettes and matches and pills for me to sneak in. On occasion we would not be strip-searched and could sneak it in.

I had issues with guys my own age so when it was time to

go to school integrated with the boys side it created some anxiety for me. I remembered how much I was teased in school by them calling me a dog and a mutt, while having fist fights with them to try to shut them up. It was a horrible time for me. As long as there were other girls in the class I would be okay. Off I went to my respective classes. By midmorning, through communicating with the others I figured out that in my next class I might be the only girl. This would not be good. I had lost a lot of my self-confidence over the past year and only felt strong when I had drugs or alcohol in me to back me up. Of course this was not allowed and although I had snuck in some pills from my mother's visit they were now all gone.

When I arrived at the class I peeked in the door in hopes that I might see another girl, even one would be okay. My eyes scanned the room and as I did I could feel all eyes upon me and chuckling in the background. Whether this was real or I was hallucinating created by my fear I don't know. All I knew was it felt real to me. I was right; there were no other girls in the room. I panicked and started to walk back to the house. One of the staff stopped me and said, "Where are you going?"

I replied defiantly, "I cannot go to that class; they are all boys in it. I can't do it."

He said, "You have to or you will have to go to the diggers." I knew the diggers would be a better option for me so I said, "That is fine, take me to the diggers and lock me up."

Normally the maximum time they would keep someone in there would be three days. By law they had to let you out for a half hour each day for fresh air. This did not happen. They kept asking me if I was ready to go back to school each day. Every day I said, "No I am not." When they would ask me why, I was embarrassed and would say because I didn't think they would understand. So I said nothing except, "I just don't want to."

This continued for seven days until finally the warden asked to speak to me and I was taken to his office. He kept badgering and badgering me to find out why I would not go back. Finally I said, "Because they are all boys in that class." The warden's face softened and he said, "Have you had problems with them before? Do they not treat you right?" At that moment he struck a chord with his soft-spoken voice and I began to cry, spilling out all my emotions to him.

The warden must have realized that whatever I had gone through before in school had a strong hold on me now. He decided this was something he could fix. A few hours later a staff member came to release me from my cell and bring me back to the group. Somehow the warden had a change of heart and arranged for me to have a different class with lots of girls in it and I was relieved.

The building I was in had an office to the front, locked doors and huge living room area, with two levels, a quiet area, and the TV area. There was a long hallway with bedrooms along each side. The good thing about this school was each girl had her own room. Then there was the deep dark basement. Well it wasn't really dark but after the events that went on down there it became known as dark. That was where the laundry room was located.

On different nights one person was assigned to stay up late and finish folding the laundry that was left. This was okay as long as Mr. Taylor was not on duty. He was an ugly man with missing teeth and what was left of them, were rotten.

He had a long, egg-shaped head and balding on top. His body was an average size and his height about five feet nine inches. Everyone cringed when he was on and they got chosen to do laundry duty. Mr. Taylor would pull favors, as they say. If he was working when visiting time was over he would let the girls bring in their drugs and cigarettes; sometimes he would even give you some and then tell you not to say anything. I would soon find out why.

It was my turn for laundry duty. I was nervous and scared because I had heard the stories. I quickly went down to finish the laundry and frantically tried to fold as quickly as I could. Hoping that I would finish before Mr. Taylor came down. Too late, there he was standing in front of me making small talk. Telling me how beautiful I was, in fact, he said that was why he let me come in with the smokes he knew my mom had given me when she visited. He promised not to tell anyone as long as I would let him feel my breasts. I knew it was a no-win situation and allowed him to fondle me both up and down. There was always another staff on duty so Mr. Taylor could not remain down there long, the only good thing about it. I returned to my room feeling completely violated by a staff member who was supposed to be there to protect me and guide me. I suppose it could have been worse I thought and everything must get better.

***

One day I decided that this was not the place for me and planned my escape, of course bringing someone along because I really wasn't that self-confident to do it on my own. Through the emergency doors, wearing my baby doll pajamas, sirens echoing across the grounds, clutching onto my clothes as hard as I could I ran and ran and ran. The friend I brought with me was Nikki from Bowmanville, the first girl I had met. Also she was one of the girls who took off with me on the camping trip as well. Nikki had a similar upbringing in the fact that she really was a good kid who just got mixed up with the wrong crowd. Not being understood at home. She said we could stay at her friend's place in Alliston. Promises of a great party at the potato festival coming up soon all sounded wonderful to me and it had to be better than where we were.

After spending the night hiding under a farmer's trailer, the coast was clear, so we ventured out. By this time we had also gotten dressed except me, I only had one shoe. I must have dropped it along the way when I was running so fiercely to escape. Oh well, I would have to do without it and decided to leave the other shoe behind as it looked a bit silly to be walking around with one shoe. Good thing it wasn't winter.

We heard some traffic noise in the far distance so we headed that way hoping to hitch a ride with a trucker. Why just a trucker you say and not a car or something else? Well, everyone knew the truckers were solid, another word for cool at the time. Usually they would pick you up no questions asked. Never expect favors in return and sometimes buy you breakfast as they did that morning. It was much safer for young girls' hitchhiking; this was a well known fact on the streets. Besides in most cases they would also be going farther. In this case it was perfect as the gentleman that stopped to pick us up did just that.

Upon arriving in Alliston, we partied at the potato festival and met all of Nikki's friends for a few days. We were getting hungry and needed a shower so Nikki decided she would go back home first. She was convinced her parents would be happy to see her and would be okay with it. Well, they were at first, until she brought me in saying this was a friend of hers that she met in training school. They were polite to my face but took Nikki in the back room and forbade her to see me. They were worried I would be a bad influence on her and told her that I had to leave. Moments later Nikki brought out the bad news and said she would find me a ride back home. I understood there wasn't anything that she could do and was grateful for the ride back to my mom's. I knew my mother would always take me in even though the situation was not always good.

A few hours later I arrived at my mother's place and was greeted with open arms. Only problem was my mother now had a boyfriend of sorts. His name was Dennis Dumont, a tall, lanky man, much older than her, somewhere in his late sixties. He was balding on top, only a few strands left, not very good teeth and rotting fingernails. A couple of his nails were big and yellow with green chunks. I remembered this the most because about one week later while I was sleeping and my mother had gone to the doctor's Dennis tried to feel my breasts. I freaked out when Dennis tried to grab me and ran out the door. Another bad male experience; it's no wonder I was becoming more distrustful of men. It just kept happening. I ran downstairs and called the police to tell them what this man had done. Once the police found out that it was my mother's boyfriend they said there was nothing they could do.

You see in those days the police and society were not as progressed as they are now with regards to these issues. I told my mother when she got home and she threw him out. Sometimes my mother could be so confident and helpful and loving, while other times she would turn on a dime. It was always when she was drinking or on pills though. When she was sober she was the type of person who would give a stranger the shirt off her back if they were in need. If only that side of her was always displayed. A few weeks later when my mom got her welfare check she bought a bottle of vodka and started drinking. At first I thought this was great, partying with my mother, until she turned. It was as if Meigan became a different person.

We argued and fought, eventually leading to Meigan calling the cops on me while I was sleeping. I was asleep in the back room with my coat on, fully clothed with shoes because the heat had been turned off for non-payment of bills. Meigan told them her daughter ran away.

When they arrived they looked around the apartment as they would normally do and found me in the bed and told me to get up. They accused me of running away because at this point they thought Meigan had custody and had not checked anything yet. I told them I did not run away and that the reason I had clothes and shoes on was that there was no heat and I was cold. They didn't believe me and thought I snuck in the back door to the bedroom. I told them that the door had a padlock from outside and explained how I could not possibly lock it from the outside. The police figured maybe I had a friend lock it for me and continued to side with my mother. I told them politely can't you see that she is just drunk and making things up. Just at that moment Meigan got up and picked up the paring knife she had on the table and charged over to me to stab me, calling me a fuckin' bitch. Seconds before the blade touched me the police stepped in and grabbed Meigan's wrist and squeezed it, releasing the knife from her hand. The police managed to calm my mother down and I agreed to go out for a while to let my mother cool down. For this reason and the fact that they believed my mother had custody the cops decided to let me stay.

While I was out I decided to call Marcia Morris to see what she was doing. Marcia knew a place where we could rent an apartment in Parkdale and said we could also find a job. So I went with Marcia and sure enough the landlord did rent to us. Of course I had to lie and say I was 16 or they wouldn't have rented it to us. This was where I met Bill Easton, Marcia's boyfriend at the time. He lived down the hall and Marcia would go to his place to hang out. He was about five foot nine then, dirty blond hair and quite hyper. That is all I'm going to tell you about Bill for now, as he will reappear in my life a few years later where we will talk about him in much more detail.

I found a job working at a factory and was paying my rent and so excited to be acting like a responsible adult. The yearning deep within for my dad to be proud of me was eating away at me. I called him to tell him how well I was doing. My stepmother answered the phone and said my father was out. While I explained how good I was doing my stepmother praised me saying how wonderful that was. She then proceeded to ask me where it was. She said she and my father would love to come to see my apartment. I was thrilled I felt I was finally doing something good and had no hesitation of giving Mavis the address. I cleaned my apartment so well that day knowing my dad and stepmother would be coming to visit.

Several hours later the buzzer rang and it was Mavis and Fred. After pretending to like the apartment and looking around they said, "It sounds like you're doing good then," and said they had to go. As they were leaving the landlord was in the hall, I was excited to be like an adult now and introduced my parents to the landlord. Mavis started freaking out of nowhere. How could you rent an apartment to an underage girl blah blah blah. I knew at this point I could not trust my parents anymore. Needless to say I had to leave my apartment.

So I had no other choice but to return to my mother's place. But that wouldn't last long because my mother again became extremely intoxicated and called the police to tell them her daughter was a runaway. She did all of this without me knowing and unexpectedly the police arrived at the door to take me away.

The police did a quick search and sure enough they found that I was reported as AWOL (escaping) from a juvenile detention center. Even though I was not too happy with the thought of going back to training school, I was somewhat relieved as I had spent several weeks with little to no food and had been constantly battling with my mother. Again I was hoping and believing there must be something better.

I only had three more months of my time left to serve anyway. I returned to Cobourg and behaved as best as I could with the knowledge I would soon be out. Those last few months were spent in counseling sessions, the staff trying to figure out what location would be best suited for me. They ran through the options with me and realized that both my parents were not a possibility, and by this point I had gained a little more independence and I liked that.

Children's Aid was the next step but I wasn't too keen on that until they mentioned an independent group home. My ears perked up as they explained that everyone there was turning sixteen or older, which at the time I was almost sixteen. They explained that everyone has their own room and there would be staff, not foster parents in charge. I kept listening intently as they mentioned each person either had to work or go to school. If you go to school you have to do chores around the house to earn an allowance. If you are working then you have to pay a nominal rent to teach you how to pay bills. Eventually when you are ready they help you find your own apartment and get you all set up. Well, perfect I thought this is exactly what I needed and agreed this would be the best option.

Little did I know, I still really hadn't dealt with any of my personal issues from the past and I would need to face this at the new location as counseling was all part of it.

CHAPTER SEVEN

STRANGE PHONE MESSAGE

1056 Bernard Street, in the Dupont area, is where I would spend the next few years of my life. What a great big old house, lots of rooms, large TV room, massive kitchen and office in the back room. Plenty of room in the back yard and the front of the house had a beautiful veranda that wrapped around its facade.

This is where I met Mindy and Sid. Mindy was a short, big-chested, large-bellied girl with long curly brown hair and glasses. Not sure of all the reasons she was there, but her mother was a whack job, an alcoholic, who was verbally abusive. Her stepfather and brother used to hold her down and rape her at age nine. Mindy's mother refused to believe this was happening, until several years later, when she wanted to kick the stepfather out. That is when she brought up the incidents and made Mindy testify in court. I didn't know at the time, but would later find out, that Mindy was a lesbian. Well no wonder, after what she had gone through. Sid was a tall, stocky girl, with lots of tattoos all over her body, and short bleached blond hair. Sid wasn't her real name; this was the name she wanted everyone to call her, even the staff. The name came from her love for the rock star, "Sid Vicious."

This group home really was a good setup. I really liked it, as I was able to have some independence, without people getting on my case. Only problem was, there were still issues deep inside me that I had not dealt with that would continue to resurface when I least expected it. In the meantime, I would try to forget about it, put it deep in the back of my mind and take that step forward.

There were two options, as I mentioned earlier, in order to qualify to stay in this group home. One was that you must go to school or work. The staff had a discussion with me to review my direction. I realized I had not completed the regular school, but that it would take too long to get ahead. The staff suggested many options for programs designed for what they called, "mature students. The programs were anywhere between nine and twelve months, and some did not require that you have a grade twelve diploma. I looked over the list and found hairdresser/hair stylist. I loved helping the girls out with their hair, trying different things, allowing my natural creativity to flow. This really excited me, so I decided I would go to Bruno's school of hair design.

Each day I would go to school all dressed up in a nice skirt or dress, hair and makeup intact. My marks were high, a clear indication of my natural talent for that industry. I met lots of new friends, straight and narrow friends, if you know what I mean. I carried on each day for months pretending to be the person I really wanted to be. Someone that society and my father could respect. But there was still a certain amount of unhappiness in my soul. Something was missing--love. And without love there always remained emptiness.

How could I forget and make this feeling go away. Each night I struggled with these thoughts. Mindy had the answer. There was always someone like Mindy out there to help steer you in another direction with promises of wonderful, glorious visions separating you from reality. And another drug I would be introduced to. The cost was cheap and the high was instantaneous. Most importantly it was legal and could be bought in a store. That was the kicker--it met all my requirements.

Mindy had purchased the items the first time and put them in her pocket. She came home, got me and we went down to the railroad tracks where we could not be seen. Although this drug was legal to buy, it was still a drug and this was a rule of the group home not to do any drugs in order to stay there. We jumped one of the flatbed boxcars that were parked on the rails for the night and Mindy pulled out a plastic bag and a tube of airplane model glue. I could not figure out how these two things could possibly do what Mindy had promised but I was willing to try. Mindy took the plastic bag and placed a small squirt of the glue in it. Then with a brief instruction telling me "to keep the opening of the bag closed to the air until you are ready so it doesn't dry out," she sucked in the air from the bag through her mouth. "Whenever you feel like you need another jolt, just place the opening near your mouth again, and inhale the fumes."

We sniffed the glue all night, experiencing one hallucination after another. At one point I was married to an Indian who I could see fully in my view. He had a long mane of feathers in his headdress. I felt so at peace, not a care in the world. Everything my friend had said came true.

Another time when we were there it was so quiet and serene by the train tracks we could hear the crickets making their clicking sounds loud and clear. I had my hair in French braids all tight to my head that night. Mindy said to me, "You look like a cricket." Well the next vision was exactly that. While the crickets creaked loudly I called out with an announcement. "All you crickets be quiet now." It went completely silent. Both of us could no longer hear the crickets. Mindy turned to me and said, "You are the mother cricket."

Night after night, week after week, we would sniff glue. By day I continued to go to hair dressing school. I needed a model for my final exam that I would have to practice on ahead of time. Someone I could do a roller set on, etc. My mother was the only one I knew that wore a roller set and had the type of hair to manipulate like that. So Mindy and I would go down to my mom's house on weekends and my mom would give us fifty cents to buy some glue, completely in total approval; anything to make her daughter happy. She was guilt-ridden from all the years of not being there for her children and this was her way of giving back.

One of the other requirements of the group home was that I must attend counseling. And guess what? The counselor came to the house so there was no way out of it. When he arrived once a week we would go to the back office to be in private from the rest of the house.

He was a short man with curly brown hair and glasses. He seemed nice enough but from my perspective, no one "especially a man" could be trusted. I had given my trust to people before only to be stabbed in the back later. So I decided I wasn't telling him anything. Week after week I could see his frustration at not getting through to me. But he was persistent and kept trying new ways to get me to talk. Finally after months had passed he finally struck a chord with me. I broke down in tears uncontrollably and began to speak about some of the issues bothering me deep down.

A few weeks later I received a phone call from my children's aid worker, since I was a permanent ward of the system and they were my legal guardians now. It was a new worker and "a man." The two things I did not deal with very well. It took me a long time to build trust with someone new. He was abrupt and stern, which raised flags for me in my internal warning system. But to top it off he said with sarcasm in his voice, "So how long are you going to need these counseling sessions for anyway? You know it's costing us money."

Well, my face started burning; I felt totally insulted and embarrassed. The wall that was just starting to come down immediately went back up in about thirty seconds. With a defensive tone I replied "It's done, I don't need it anymore." When the counselor showed up that week all excited knowing they had finally made some progress he was greeted by an angry, completely emotionally-shut-down girl with a defensive attitude in her voice. "Didn't you hear, I told them these sessions are done? They said it's costing them money and how long is this going to take anyway? So I don't want to cost anyone money. So we're done." And I walked out.

The counselor was angry at the Children's Aid Society because he was finally making progress after so many months and then they go and tell me something like that. He got on the phone right away and tried to change their decision. It really wouldn't have mattered anyway because my wall was even higher than it was when we first started. There was no going back.

I continued to battle my demons by myself every day and now it was my weight that seemed to be in the forefront. I had heard about a diet called "Scarsdale diet." I purchased the book and began altering my food consumption. The more I looked in the mirror the fatter I became, in my eyes, anyway. Soon I altered the diet and stopped eating the meat in it. Within no time I became anorexic. My bones protruded out of my neckline, while my clothes just hung on me like baggy rags. Even though people kept mentioning how skinny I was, to me I was still fat. Months later I was able to come to my senses and pull myself out of it after seeing a picture of myself. I really don't remember if that was the whole reason or the fact that I prayed and prayed to God to help me, to save me from my suffering. He always answered my prayers no matter what situation I was in. It didn't always happen right away but I truly believed in my heart that he would save me. Or again was it my belief system that there is always something better that carried me through as this always seemed to be prominent in my mind.

***

It wasn't long after that I decided I was ready to go on my own. I was over sixteen and with this group home there was a program that helped you pay your rent until you found work. Sid and I decided to rent an apartment together. We found a nice new building on College Street by Grace Street. It was a one-bedroom but with no door on it, separated only by one wall right across from the bathroom. There was a pretty large living room and small kitchenette attached. It was perfect, so we packed our things and said our goodbyes while venturing off to independence.

I remembered a phone message I had received when I first arrived in the group home, about one week in. It was that a man named Donavan Richard called and asked to have me call him at the Don Jail. At the time I discussed it with my friends and had no recollection of Donavan Richard nor did I know anyone in the Don Jail so I quickly put it out of my mind and had forgotten about it.

Until one night while Sid and I were enjoying our new apartment and me with only a few months left to complete my course the topic came up. We discussed this unusual message I had received nine months prior. Sid was intrigued and said, "You should call, at least to see who it is. Aren't you curious?" Now that the topic was in the forefront I couldn't let it out of my mind. It was driving me crazy not knowing. So with little coercion I decided to call the Don Jail. A man answered the phone and I asked to speak to Donavan Richard. The man asked, "Is he a guard or an inmate?" I explained that I did not know and that I had just received this message to call him. So the man looked on the system for a guard with that name first and said there are no guards with that name. Then he checked the inmate records. There were no inmates with that name either. He suggested calling the West Detention Center as most inmates usually get moved there since the Don Jail was only a temporary holding facility.

With Sid egging me on I called the West Detention Center. Lo and behold there was a Donavan Richard there as an inmate. The man on the phone explained the visiting hours and days and said the inmates are not allowed to take phone calls.

After I hung up the phone we were freaking out. "How can this be? Who is this guy? How did he get your number? Especially at the group home?" We went on and on. Finally I decided I couldn't take it anymore, I just had to know. Sid agreed to take the long bus trip with me to the jail.

When we arrived at the front desk they said, "Only one visitor allowed and you need to show your ID and sign in." My heart was racing; this was crazy and totally out there. The excitement of adventure took me over completely. After having my purse checked and going through a metal detector they took me into a visiting room. There were a group of others also going in. I stood back as everyone entered. I thought maybe I would recognize this person as they came out. Both the inmates and the visitors were entering at the same time. They were separated by half a wall and a bulletproof Plexiglas window. Below the window was a table and stool. Each space had barriers on the left and right of the table to block off the voices of the people sitting next to you. Lastly, there was a telephone handset receiver only one on each side. As the inmates and visitors saw each other they showed signs of recognition and would sit in the seat opposite. I was frantically scanning the inmates hoping to have some sort of recollection, but nothing. Finally, there was all but one inmate left to be seated; slowly he sat down in the last space available in front of me. He was a very tall black man who seemed to recognize me at first glance. However I had no memory of this man at all. I sat down and we picked up the phone in unison and I said, "Donavan Richard?"

"Yes," he said.

I shouted out, "I don't know you."

Donavan agreed but said, "You do look familiar; you look a lot like my ex-girlfriend, Kim."

I proceeded to tell him that I received a message from him nine months earlier to call him at the Don Jail. Then Donavan explained that he met a man in jail who knew me and said I would help him with his case if I could. That I was a solid person and someone you could rely on. This statement made me feel good knowing that people thought I was a good person. We talked for a half hour until visiting hours were over. Donavan told me all about his charges and that he was falsely accused and pleaded for my help. When I asked, "What do you need me to do?" he replied, "I will be in touch."

Later I was contacted by a priest in the west end of the city who said he had a letter from Donavan for me to pick up. Again curious, I went to pick up the letter. As the priest passed me the letter he said, "You tell Donavan that this is the last time, I can't be doing this." Here is how the letter read...

Hi Michele;

No, I don't need glasses, I was sitting there dumbfounded because you look so much like my ex and when you have been in jail this long trying to hold on to your sanity and someone calls you out of your cage and that someone looks almost identical to your lover, who flew off to Vancouver "because the pigs that busted you wouldn't leave her alone and there is this voice on the other end of the phone saying over and over, are you Donavan Richard?" You're bound to freak for second and just sit there staring excuse me if I seemed ignorant, I truly am not! I will be calling to get your address so that I can mail this and I want you to know that I am thankful to you and Sid for coming out to see me, no matter if it was only out of boredom.

I will tell you about me, my name is Nathan Donavan Richards (not Richard) I am from Chicago, but was raised up in Los Angeles. I am twenty seven and never looked and felt so bad in my life! (Smile) the important thing to tell you is that I am not a liar or pretender about anything I have said to you or anything that I will ever say. I am the type of person whose friends last forever and try not to leave my enemies around for long enough to discuss! A realist, I am! A loser "I am not: I do believe in money, getting high and traveling: but beyond my regular habits; as a person I am always firstly interested in a solid old lady. At this point in my life, I don't have that, for the first time since I was twelve. I don't have an old lady. Oh, I am well equipped physically and mentally to handle all of the street games, therefore giving a fuck has never been and will never be a problem for me. I don't even need to look for pussy anymore, but I am looking like crazy for someone to go through life with and truly Michele, I am the type of person if I can't find the magic of love and the bond of togetherness that two people get together and make for themselves, dealing with the woman is not much worth the effort to me.

For all of the shit we go through and take off other people love you see is the only real payoff. And that has to be the kind of love that takes each person where they need to go-together. See you too have gone through your motions with the pigs and the piggish people, which are sometimes worse than the pigs themselves. There is no sense in my attempting to manipulate you about the matter. I am a con artist!, a fraud artist and a dope smuggler. Not into pimping because the money is too slow and for a truly smart man that is giving just a little bit more than money is worth, for in the long run the whore and the pimp is the tricks in the booths. Since I know that I am not into that: I really liked you not only your looks but also your thoughts and your opinion on different matters. I know that we met in a strange way but that is the best way. There are no games to play, if you think that you liked me enough and if you want an old man who soars like an eagle and doesn't flop like a turkey, let me know.

You do not have to agree unless you agree, we can remain friends and I would be grateful for the favor you might do for me concerning my trial and showing at court, but I might as well tell you what is on my mind. Now tell me what is on yours? As for when you show for my trial get this into your head, do not talk to any cops, if they question you in casual conversation at court, do not talk about me, they will only be fishing to find out how long we know each other and just what you might be testifying to! Which is something that is very easy to handle, I will not put you in a position for perjury or any type of charges yourself. So do not worry about that! I will think of you first before I would ask you to take the stand for me!

First of all, get this through your head, when you walk into the courtroom, everyone in there is going to think that you are my ex. Even the people who have sat right across the table from her and have known her for years. She's also 19! And identical to you, now would I take a chance like that if I did not know what I was talking about? No, I would not! Which means they are truly going to be scared shitless, for if she was around, they would not be in town let alone at court! But you have to know what these people look like! Tim Davis-19-bright red Afro-Irish, Mona Davis-long black hair-17- These two are my people, they are sister and brother, they will be on my side 100%. Chelsea Christensen

-Frizzy blond hair-19, Denise Michaels -27-black straight hair-French-even in accident. Now the rat is Randy O'Halleran-long brown hair wearing glasses-18.

Now write this stuff on another sheet of paper, see if you can get each name and identify it in your head ask Sid to help you. But do not let anyone else know what you are working on. You never know who is taking what in! Now once you have this down in your head, just go to court and you and Sid just move around the area like normal people, looking at them! Each time you get a chance, just say, I hope you get it straight! Do not threaten or intimidate, just have that look in your eyes! Those exact words Michele, nothing more! Simply, I hope you get it straight!

My lawyer is a black guy, Chuck River. Go up to him and tell him, (I will point them out to you at court) so stick close to the prison box so you can talk to me! Tell him that you are one of my witnesses and he must bring you down stairs to visit with me, (this can be done in the High Court) insist that he does this! (No phones) when you tell me that you have spotted each of them and gotten this across to them remember when they see you they are going to say hey Kim that's who they will think you are! Just go shhh! With your finger to your mouth to indicate to not call you or talk to you! When I see you again, hopefully on that day I will tell you the next move!

Sid will take the stand and testify to the fact that Donavan has her phone number in his phonebook. Right after he went to jail, she started to get phone calls at all hours of the night every night, from people wanting to buy narcotics, and asking her when did she get back from Jamaica. Since she does not use narcotics and has never been to Jamaica, she did not know what was going on, this kept up from the middle of May till the middle of August, she kept hanging up and telling them they have the wrong number. But they kept calling back! One night a guy called and said, "can I come over and get some dope, I got the money", and "Donavan sent me." Since she knew Donavan was in jail plus the fact that she is not that type of person, she became afraid and called one of her friends! Who also knew Donavan, this girl (any name) told Sid that Donavan's address book was with the police and everyone's name in the book was getting the same kind of phone calls, that she was lucky, some people had their doors kicked in.

Sid is going to be asked tricky questions like do you do narcotics? (A.) no! Does Donavan do narcotics? (B.) not that I know about! How long have you known Donavan (A.) ever since he came from Chicago in November of 1979. Where did he live? In a basement apartment at 204 Barton Street, one block north of Christie subway. He moved in middle of February 19. Did not see him after that! How did you come to know this man? He is a photographer and he was teaching me how to use cameras! (Which is true) we met at the floating world disco! And became friends and saw each other whenever we wanted. (Can't remember any exact times)

"Important" do you know any of his co-accused the people here today!

(Answer)

No, but I did know some people who did not have a home was supposed to be living with him. I told him to kick them out and let them earn their own way. But he was too soft hearted and kept saying, where can they go in the middle of the winter? So I said, to hell with that! And stopped seeing him! That is what Sid is to say: each time that they tried to make me look like a bad guy, tell her to say, no that is not Donavan!

Michele do you think that you can get this together for me without messing it up? If you can more than likely I will walk! Please stay available for me to reach you by phone and try to make it to each court date, it will go on from day to day, all of the preliminaries are passed me. The more I think about you, the more I like you! Let's go to California! (Smile)

Affectionately Donavan

Keep in mind that I was extremely naïve. I also truly wanted to help people. From childhood I always stuck up for the underdog. Even though I was prepared to go to court and help Donavan there was no interest in dating him. I really believed he was innocent like the stories I had been told before from my friends and I knew sometimes people were falsely accused by the police. For two and a half weeks I skipped hairdressing school to attend court and have meetings with Donavan. This was all very exciting and adventurous to me and I played along exactly as he mentioned in the letter. The people he said would recognize me as Kim did. This was like acting for me, which I loved, but most importantly according to Donavan I was the only one who could help him get out of jail.

Everything was going as planned until two things happened. First the Children's Aid Society who was supporting me while I was in school, threatened to cut me off. They had been notified that I had not been in school for the past two weeks. They gave me an ultimatum and said, "You either go back to school tomorrow or we cut you off financially and you are on your own." Secondly, the police arrived the day before to give their testimony. All eyes were on me. I suddenly realized that these cops looked very familiar. When they announced that they were from Fourteen Division where I had been brought into the station over and over again I figured they must know me. How could I possibly go up on the stand and say I was Kim if these cops knew me. They would know I was lying and I would be charged with perjury. Not only that, I would lose my apartment and my hairdressing status. It was like a wake-up call--a light went on in my head and I realized this was not a good idea.

Next day I returned to school and went on to complete the course. Each day I would check the newspaper and watch the news to see what happened with Donavan's case. I was still curious. The announcement was made after three weeks of trial Donavan Richards was sentenced to three years in a federal penitentiary. When I heard that I was relieved that I had come to my senses or I might have been joining him there. It was as if my guardian angels were always watching out for me, trying to give me messages over and over again. My mind was so blocked with alcohol and drugs I could not recognize or see the signs. As a last resort my angels had to contact the Children's Aid Society to get through to me. What a story I would tell my children one day, almost unbelievable but it's true. I never heard from Donavan after that day, it was as if the whole thing never happened.

***

I moved on with my life. After completing my hairdressing course which I passed with flying colors I had to take a final exam in order to get my license. When that day arrived, my model, who was my mother that I had practiced on all these months and passed the school exam with, was wasted, totally inebriated. It took months to set up this appointment with the government to do the test and if you didn't show, you failed. I was devastated. My mother knew how important this was to me. It seemed that every time I tried to get ahead something would always come in the way to make me fail. I cried and cried that day and through the night. My only escape that I knew could help me forget was drugs and of course men.

I still did not have an understanding of the true meaning of love. At this point although I had intercourse numerous times it was always to their pleasure. I didn't even know what an orgasm was but had a pretty good idea how to fake it. This was all I knew about love and figured this must be it. As each encounter passed I still felt unsatisfied; empty inside.

One night I decided to confide in Sid. While Sid was talking about how wonderful coming was or having an orgasm I spoke up and said, "It is no big deal, why do you keep saying it is so special?" Sid figured out that I probably had not had an orgasm before. She began to explain to me how it felt and what happens to your body. As I listened intently I realized that was not what I remember ever happening. Sid also talked about masturbating, another term I knew nothing about. She was shocked to find out that I had never done this. For some reason probably due to what happened to me when I was four years old. I felt that was something dirty and did not feel comfortable doing it. Sid relayed to me that I was missing the best part. She also mentioned they write about it in the books, and threw one of them on the bed beside me.

That night Sid had a date with some guy and went out. I had been drinking and smoking pot with her most of the day and planned to retire early. I lied there tossing and turning, my mind racing a mile a minute like it usually did, especially before bed. As I rolled over to the other side I saw the book Sid had thrown there in our earlier conversation. I picked up the book and started reading. I became so engrossed in this book I couldn't put it down. Of course I got to the part where the girl was masturbating I put the book down and the rest of it was history.

The next morning I felt like a brand-new woman, enlightened to new heights. When Sid woke up I told her all about it gleaming with excitement I wanted to shout it out to the world, but quickly realized by the look on Sid's face that I needed to be cool and calm down. That was the last I spoke of it.

I had a job for a short time at Magic Cuts just before my exam was to happen. When I couldn't complete the exam due to my mother's state I did not feel happy at that job anymore. All I would be doing the rest of my life was sweeping floors and washing hair without having my license. They did give me an option to redo the test but I could not bear the disappointment of my mother not being there for me again. And the hours of practice I had done with her I could not possibly find a new model in time. I needed to find an alternative way to survive and the search began.

CHAPTER EIGHT

PREDATORS

All the street smart, government-savvy people that lived in the building quickly gave me the rundown on how they could sit at home and get paid for not working. "Welfare 101." I followed their instructions to apply and got my first check. This was great, I thought, "I can party every day and not have to work." And that is what I did. It was getting a bit boring for me though. I was feeling lonely and was hoping I would meet someone I could be with on a more permanent basis.

While I was in hairdressing school and had just moved into the apartment I had met a police officer. Of course I lied about my age because I was only sixteen at the time, but I was sure if he really wanted to know he would have found out the truth. Instead he ignored that because he wanted something else that would not be legal for a cop to do on the job anyway. I won't get into too much detail but horrifyingly enough he would take me places in his car after making me get all dressed up thinking I was going on a real date and make me perform indecent acts on him.

Chalk another one up to my list of men who weren't so nice.

The more I thought about it, the more I thought it must be my fault. How could all these men doing the same things be the problem? I am only one; no one else seems to have this problem, I thought. Other people have real boyfriends. I continued to beat myself up chanting, "I am a horrible person, that's why people treat me this way. God is punishing me for something I did." My young mind could take no more. No matter how hard I tried I always got shot down, this was the day my self-esteem left the building. On the outside I seemed the same but inside I blamed myself for my whole life's mess. I prayed and prayed for God to save me, pull me out of this depression. God always answered my prayers and this time was no different.

A few days later one of the guys in the building said, "There's a new guy just moved in down the hall and he has a keyboard with a sound system. It's awesome you should check it out. He has some beer too. Let's all go over." Great; some excitement, I thought and gladly went with everyone to this new guy's place.

As I entered as the last one in the door I looked through the group to find this guy with a keyboard. I could hear everyone introducing themselves in front of me seeming to shake his hand. I heard his name--Bill. The crowd slowly moved aside and it was my turn to meet this man. When I looked up and saw his face I thought he looked really familiar, but could not place it at the time.

Bill was really cute. Not really tall but taller than me; about five-foot-nine, blonde hair, shoulder length, feathered back and big blue eyes. He was thin, not too thin, nice small butt and good muscles on his arms. He kept checking me out on the sly while he was showing everyone what the keyboard could do. I was probably the most interested in this keyboard anyway. It allowed for creative expression and this was a strong part of who I was. So aside from me thinking Bill was hot, I really did enjoy the whole keyboard thing. Everyone shared a joint and Bill continued to play strange sounds on the keyboard. It was like trains rolling on the rails, horns tooting, bird noises, gun sounds; it was incredible--one of the first of its kind.

Slowly the crowd filtered out and back to their apartments. I was about to leave too when Bill said, "Why don't you stay? I can show you how to use the keyboard." It really didn't take much convincing for me to stay since I already had the hots for him. Once the door was closed Bill said, "I have met you before, you are friends with Marcia Morris." Then I realized who he was, he used to date my friend Marcia. "Oh no," I thought, "what if he is still dating Marcia?" She would be pissed off if she thought I was after her man. So I spoke up, "You are Marcia's boyfriend--is she here?"

He said, "No she is crazy, I broke up with her a long time ago. I never really liked her that much but she kept stalking me." He continued to tell me that he was single and all about himself and what type of person he was. We laughed, played the keyboard and smoked dope talking all night. I didn't want to leave nor did Bill want me to leave. Our shoulders would touch as Bill showed which buttons to push on the keyboard. Sitting so close we could feel each other's heartbeats. The emotions and hormones were exploding in the room; both of us could feel it. Bill repeatedly told me how beautiful I was and that he was looking for a steady girlfriend. I practically melted in his arms but clearly showing him my tough exterior. Intrigued by this, Bill couldn't resist and leaned over to put his hands behind my neck, pulled me close and kissed me so deeply I felt like I blacked out. It seemed as though firecrackers shot off around us. I regained my composure and prepared to leave, figuring I should not be so easy this time and play hard to get.

As I left I said, "It was nice meeting you." Bill stopped me at the door and said, "I really enjoyed your company and the kiss." I looked at him with a twinkle in my eye and a half-cocked smile and with a soft sexy voice whispered, "I had a really good time too."

He asked me, "When will I see you again?" I replied with my apartment number just down the hall.

 "Why don't you come over for dinner tomorrow night," Bill said. "I can cook, I am really good."

"Sure; what time," I replied.

Exuding pure confidence Bill said, "How about six p.m.?"

"Okay, sounds good." I held my composure until I got back to my apartment. Then I let it all out. I was so excited, this guy was hot and he liked me, sounded like for more than just sex.

The romance began and continued for months; I finally had a serious boyfriend and was proud of it. It is the Aries nature to give her loyalties to one man and one man only, and I was an Aries. I met Bill's parents and I really liked them. Bill's dad was a short stocky man with gray hair and not much on top. He seemed a bit mean at times and distant. I didn't think he liked me for some reason. Bill's mother, however, absolutely loved me. Sometimes even more than her own son you will find out later by her actions. She was tall, thin, with very long straight light brown hair down to her butt. She had a hard face that had suffered years of stress and cigarettes. Her voice was deep and harsh, sort of raspy, with a foul tongue inside. She was a "curse in your face" woman with a heart of gold inside. I think she liked me so much because we were a lot alike in some respects. She probably knew her son was growing up in his dad's footsteps and thought poor Michele would be caught in the line of fire just like her.

At this point I only saw a small snippet of Bill's aggression; nothing too serious that would raise concerns. Now that I had met Bill's mother my eyes would soon be a little wider. First opportunity Bill's mom had to talk with me alone she confided in me, telling me that when she was young her husband hit her. Not so much now but it changed who she was. Muriel (Bill's mom) explained to me that even though she loved her son deeply that he was much like his father. She felt she owed it to me to give me the guidance to save my life since she did not save her own. I at this point did not believe Bill could ever hurt me. He loved me. But I was bright and quizzical and listened intently to all Muriel said, storing it in my brain for future reference.

For some reason Muriel never left the house, you could always find her in the kitchen smoking and drinking tea. Not sure of the real story how that started but I have a pretty good guess. Her husband was so jealous whenever they went out that he would falsely accuse her of looking at other men. Eventually it became easier and less hassle for her just to stay home and avoid confrontation. Over time, her lack of outside human contact and its surroundings became fearful to her.

I remember one day when Muriel's cousin had passed away and she had to go to the funeral. She was a mess, shaking, eyes wide open, full of tears saying, "I can't do this, I don't want to go out." With the support and coercion of her husband, Bill Senior, she managed to leave the house. Within forty-five minutes she was back almost having a breakdown. She had several drinks and some pills to calm her down and slept for a couple of days. Muriel had made me promise that I would never let Billy (Bill) beat me, and to always stand up for myself. Confidently I promised, not realizing what was to come. Muriel was another person whose words of wisdom would give me power in the years to come. Although at the time I was not aware of this.

It began first with an argument, loud yelling, swearing and accusations, always, always, containing manipulative twisted sentences. The louder Bill yelled the less I could hear. It was as if an internal mechanism automatically turned down the sound in my head to protect me. Whatever pieces of information I heard it did not make sense. The more he spoke the more I blamed myself. "It must be my fault he is so angry, what did I do? Why is this always happening to me?" Rampant thoughts of self-degradation scattered through my brain. By the time he was finished I had convinced myself with his help that I was at fault. I would try harder next time to observe the happenings prior so that I could defend myself in an argument.

That is exactly what I did a few days later. Yes, I stood up for myself knowing I was armored with the facts. Raising my voice in defense shouting out all the reasons why Bill was wrong and I was right. As my words lingered in the air almost in slow motion they were surrounded by black clouds looming in from above. In that moment silence fell upon my ears. I could see the blood pumping through Bill's veins, strengthening his being. As the blood reached his face it became crimson red and his eyes began to bulge as the muscles clenched in his cheeks. Then "whack" Bill punched me right in the face near my eye. Suddenly all the anger stopped. I held my face in complete shock. I could not believe this man that is supposed to love me had caused me such pain. Many thoughts ran through my mind as the tears poured down my cheeks. The tears came from the sadness, not the pain.

All the memories of my childhood arose telling me I was a bad girl. I would never amount to anything. Like a schizophrenic Bill snapped right out of his anger and became this caring, loving, sorrowful man. "Oh, Michele please forgive me," he said as he gently placed his hand on mine. On and on and on he went about how he didn't know what happened to him that he lost his temper and "it will never happen again." That was the side of him that I loved and cared for. I convinced myself that maybe he wouldn't do this again and that it probably was my fault anyway.

This was the beginning of my self-destructive life of abuse. Bill continued to find reasons to beat me, reasons I at first did not believe were true. The first excuses all had to do with our friends and family and where we lived. One day I went to go see Bill's mom to talk about his behavior. I knew his mom would understand and maybe she could help. Bill followed me there frantically hoping to stop me from speaking to his mother. Muriel locked the door and would not let him in. She knew her son planned to hurt me and felt she needed to protect me from this since no one was there for her. Bill went crazy, banging and smashing at the door. "I am going to fuckin' kill you. How dare you go see my mother?" He cursed and swore at his mother calling her a traitor. She told him if he did not leave she would call the police. He knew this was the last thing he wanted and left the area.

I was even more afraid now because I knew when I eventually did see him he would be even angrier than ever. After hours of talking with Muriel she suggested I leave her son. She told me of all the times Bill's father beat her. She felt her son had grown up just like his dad and would not change. I took all of this into account and went back to pack my things and leave. When I got there Bill was down the hall at his friend's house drinking beer. I knew this would not be good and tried quickly to pack my things and get out. Moments later Bill came through the door. I froze and looked at him not knowing what to expect. He put on a nice calm face and said how sorry he was. That he could see that I was packing as if to leave.

He pleaded with me not to go. When I continued to say I was leaving I could see his face changing like it did before when he beat me. I thought quickly and figured if I changed my story and made him believe I would now stay then when he was out I could get away safely. Bill was pretty smart and had a feeling I was faking it. So we talked and talked over how we both felt.

Bill put an understanding face on and said, "If you want to leave, you can leave, I will understand." I knew immediately this must be a trick. So I kept telling him I would stay feeling him out. Finally after an hour or so I started getting tired and thought maybe he was telling the truth and he had come to his senses. I finally said, "Yes, I do want to go," and Bill said, "Okay I will get your purse for you (that he hid in the refrigerator because he felt I would not leave without it)." My heart raced with excitement and nervousness at the same time as he brought the purse towards me. The purse never reached my hand. He smashed me in the head with it and threw it aside and began beating me over and over again. Closed fisted punches to my face and kicking my body. As I lay crying bleeding and bruised on the floor he informed me that I was not going anywhere. That he would leave the door open and he would be right next door at his friend's house listening. And if I tried to escape he would make sure I regretted it.

I laid there for hours while Bill continued drinking next door. He would pop in every now and then to make sure I didn't leave. I finally couldn't take it anymore. After three days of being held captive I knew that at the end of the night he would beat me again because he would be more wasted. I needed a plan; I could not leave from the front door as Bill might see me or hear me. The only way out was through the window, but I would need to open it quietly so he would not get suspicious. I had no shoes because Bill took them next door as another deterrent for me leaving.

I slowly eased open the window, my heart racing a mile a minute, and climbed up on a chair and crawled out the window. Feet covered in socks, only purse in hand, I ran as fast as I could. It was the middle of winter with snow covering the ground but I didn't care, I knew the only way to save my life was to leave. I ran without looking back about seven kilometers down the road to my mother's place.

When I got upstairs I locked all the doors and turned out all the lights. After explaining everything to my mother and my mother's friend, Art, we all sat quietly. Bang, bang, bang, we could hear him downstairs trying to get in. Everyone was silent. He continued banging, yelling out profanities, threatening to kill us all. Bill then went around to the back and began yelling up.

My mom had long since called the police. When Bill was around the back Art decided he would try to leave to go home across the street. He was shaking he was so terrified that Bill might get in to kill us. So he quickly ran downstairs and out the front door and across the street. Bill saw him and yelled, "I see you; I am going to kill you too." Then the police finally arrived.

Bill was completely out of control and was holding a large stick by this time. Two cruisers pulled up and surrounded him. They took him down with their billies, handcuffed him, and stuffed him in the car. The whole time my mother and I watched from the window as Bill screamed out, "I am going to fuckin' kill you when I get out, bitch."

When I showed up the next day for court Bill's dad was there to bail him out. He was so angry at me he turned and gave me a really dirty look. I thought about all the times Bill was nice to me and started to feel guilty. He wasn't drinking now and he had such a sorrowful, sad face on that I could not go through with it. I dropped the charges. Bill was so grateful and told me how much he loved me. He convinced me that the problems we had were due to our respective families and friends and if we moved away we could start a new life. So that is what we did. We packed our bags and took a train to Vancouver. Our plan was to find a place and job and start a new life together.

It was an exciting adventure, I thought. Everything Bill had said seemed to make sense. This had to be the answer to our happiness. The first part of the train ride was great, until Bill found out where the bar car was. We sat down and had drinks. I was facing Bill in the last booth and behind him was a wall. Bill had a jealous rage that would come out every now and then especially when he was drinking. There was a guy sitting in a booth about three spots behind me. Bill kept accusing me of looking at him. In his crazed state he didn't realize that I had not moved my head at all and had only been looking at him and the wall behind him since we sat down. Knowing what he was like I didn't dare look around. It didn't matter though; his mind had control of what he would see, even if it wasn't there. He began getting abusive swearing at me and calling me names. Then he reached over and grabbed me by the shirt yanking me towards his face, gritting his teeth and threatening to kill me right there.

At that moment the bartender and the people in the car escorted him out. I could not stop crying, I was so embarrassed and scared for my life. What had I done taking this trip? The people behind me and the bartender were so caring. They said, "Don't worry; you can stay here. We won't let him hurt you." They were such comforting words. I stayed in the bar car for quite a while, then once I knew Bill was asleep I headed back to my seat. I knew once he woke up he would be sober and thinking straight and all that aggression would be forgotten at least for the time being.

After a three-and-a-half-day train ride we arrived in Vancouver city. We needed somewhere to stay while looking for an apartment and job so we rented a room at the St. Regis Hotel downtown temporarily. After a few days of looking first for a job we were disappointed. It seemed the jobs that were available needed more experience than we had. Both of us did not handle rejection very well and chose to have a few drinks one night.

Bill came up with a crazy plan that I could be a prostitute a few times to get some money. I was not interested in this at all and did everything in my power to convey this message to him. He refused to listen and took me to a street not too far from the hotel where there were other street workers. Well that scheme didn't work out too well because the people on the street got angry. They said this is our territory and if you don't want something bad to happen to you then you will leave now.

Bill had such attitude and with a few drinks in him he was worse. He was getting his back up wanting to start a fight. I did not want to do this anyway, especially knowing how possessive and jealous Bill was, I quickly convinced him to go back to the hotel with me. It was like Bill was always testing my love for him. He just wanted to see if I would even consider it by taking me there. I on the other hand was so afraid of Bill when he was in this state I did not want to fight with him or get him annoyed so I went along not knowing what else to do.

When Bill got back to the room he drank some more. In no time he was quite wasted and began getting agitated. When he was out earlier he had bought a pellet gun, which was illegal in Ontario but not in British Columbia. He loaded the pellet gun and opened up the window and began firing shots at the pigeons. Even though I did not care that much for pigeons I was not cruel and did not want to see them hurt. I pleaded with him to stop. The more I pleaded the more he wanted to shoot them. No one was going to tell him what to do.

Then some other people whose rooms also backed onto the laneway started looking out. One guy thought he was shooting at him and started swearing saying he was going to come over there and kill him and pulled out a real gun. I quickly pulled Bill towards me and closed the window and curtains. Bill was pissed and started shooting the pellet gun at me. I tried to block the shots but there were too many. Each pellet that hit me shot a stinging burning feeling throughout my body. I cried out, "Please stop, Bill." The more I cried the more he shot at me, almost sadistically enjoying the pain he was inflicting upon me.

When he felt he had enough from me he left the room and said he was going to find the guy that mouthed off. When the coast was clear I ran out of the room to the front desk crying. I told them my boyfriend was shooting at me with a pellet gun and I feared for my life. They immediately called the police. A short time later two officers arrived to question me. I relayed the whole story to them in the midst of my tears. When it was all over they responded with a statement I would never forget. "Since he is your boyfriend there is nothing we can do."

I then asked, "So it is okay for him to beat me?"

"This is considered domestic and you need to deal with it amongst yourselves." So there I was abandoned in a strange city with a maniac that the police basically condoned his behavior and refused to help. Scared and alone fearing for my life I decided to go back home. I packed my things, left the hotel and took a cab to the train station.

When I returned to Toronto I begged and pleaded for my apartment back but it had already been rented. I knew I wouldn't be able to stay with my mother very long for a number of reasons, but most importantly, Bill would look for me there. Quite frankly I was fed up of being abused by him and was not going back. .

CHAPTER NINE

BELIEF & POWER

While at my mother's I made a few phone calls. One of them was to my old friend Mindy. Her mother had since kicked out her abusive stepfather and was running a rooming house. Mindy convinced her mother to let me rent one of the rooms. There were a lot of old derelicts renting there who were all men.

Mindy and I became good party buddies. Mindy would take me to gay bars since she herself was lesbian. I was so frustrated and angry with men after my experience with Bill I thought maybe I should be a lesbian and forget about men altogether. After months of these experiences and one steady girlfriend I decided this was not what I really wanted. Mindy and I regularly hung out at the Edgewater Hotel. I made some new friends there and soon parted ways with Mindy.

There were a few incidents that occurred that helped me to make this decision. One night Mindy and I went out to sniff glue. I was a bit slow getting started so this was the first time I observed what it did to a person. Mindy started slurring her words and talking all crazy about things that weren't there. This scared me because I thought this is how I must look when I sniff glue. I waited until Mindy was finished, then took her home with a plan to talk to her the next morning.

When Mindy woke up the next day I explained to her how messed up she was and that I decided not to sniff glue anymore. Mindy reluctantly said she would no longer do this either. I had my doubts about Mindy's quick response. A few days later Mindy was back on it. She was dealing with lots of depression and Mindy had cut her wrists many times, always talking about wanting to die. Now I had also cut my wrist when I was with Bill and had to be taken to the hospital and stitched up. I was dealing with so much turmoil up to that point that I no longer wanted to live being beaten all the time by Bill. But somehow after leaving Bill I knew deep down inside that I had a little more fight left in me.

Mindy said, "How can I kill myself?" day in and day out. "If I only had a lot of pills to take, I could overdose." I couldn't take it anymore listening to this so I called her bluff. I told Mindy that my mother had a lot of pills at her house and took her over there. My mother was out at the time so we broke into her medicine cabinet and I passed Mindy the pills. Mindy then wrote a suicide note to take with her and decided to leave all her identification with me. She opened the bottle and swallowed about twenty chlorpromazine nerve pills and stopped. I said, "That is not enough, if you really want to die you have to take them all." Secretly I was hoping Mindy would snap out of this suicide thing and not continue. But she really did not want to live being so deeply unhappy with her life and took all of the rest.

I started to panic. "You can't die here or they will think I had something to do with it." Mindy said, "Just take me to the park and leave me there." Off we went to the Dufferin Park where we sat on a bench for about an hour. Mindy became delirious and tired. I told her to lie down under the picnic table. Once she was no longer coherent I left and went home. I was sad for her but realized that there really was nothing I could do. People choose to live and if she was willing to give that up nothing could stop her.

Somehow later that night, completely unconscious, Mindy managed to stagger out from under the table and wandered to the street where a police officer saw her and took her to the hospital. So I guess deep down within her soul she didn't really want to die. Months later I ran into her and gave her the identification back. At that point I had moved on to a different group of friends and decided Mindy was too negative to be around. It was hard enough for me to keep positive with all the things going on in my life, let alone adding another person like that to the picture.

The Edgewater hotel was my favorite drinking establishment and, wow, a lot happened there. It was a time in my life where I wanted to forget about my family. They turned their backs on me, all but my sister Jenny. My friends became my real family; they were there for me through thick and thin, or so I thought. Between friends and boyfriends I seemed to always have someone with me. I prayed a lot and asked God to help me. It seemed over and over again even though I had people around me I still felt alone. So alone I wanted to die. Each time one of my boyfriends would betray or hurt me it was like a bad spirit jumping out of my body and taking control.

In those days women didn't play pool, there was something

about it that bothered me. I had a real attitude from childhood that stood very strongly on this matter. Whenever I was told I couldn't do something, especially because I was female, this made me want to do it even more just to prove them wrong. I truly believed that people could do anything they set their minds to, no matter what the gender. And that is exactly what I intended to do with regards to billiards.

Jerry Murphy, a tall, thin, good-looking man was at the table beating the pants off everyone who came close. I sat across the room watching intently at his moves. Everything about him was sexy. His whole demeanor captured my attention. On occasion he would look my way with his hands holding the cue in front of his genitals, one foot forward leaning back, head tilted towards his chin almost resting on his chest, he raised his head slightly and his deep blue eyes met mine. Whoa, what power, I quickly looked away and raised my nose in the air slightly as if to say I am too good for you. This was a game I would play like cat and mouse. Knowing full well this would make him want me more, showing him gestures to say otherwise.

This game went on for about an hour. I would take short trips to the bar to flaunt what I had even more. Tight jeans with a nice round butt, body tight tank top with laced up front. My muscular body displayed to the masses as I returned to my seat with shots of tequila. Now, he knew I was tough and he racked his brain for a way to get to my heart.

After all the players had been beaten and he was alone at the pool table my friend takes her cue and goes to the ladies room, leaving the area wide open for this man to approach. My heart started racing as I saw this hunk through the corner of my eye slowly approaching. What do I say? No time to think about that; he is here, I thought. His voice deep, sexy, and powerful said, "Do you want to play," and proceeded to pass me the pool cue. I looked up with this shy smile and blushing cheeks and said innocently, "I would love to but I don't know how to play." Great lead-in, Michele, you are genius, I chanted in my mind. Jerry said with a gentle voice as he reached his hand out for mine, "That's okay, I can teach you." I was thrilled. Not only did I have a chance to get to know this mysterious man who seemed to have captured my heart, but I would also have an opportunity to learn how to play pool from the best. This is great I thought, I always wanted to learn but was too nervous to go up there and make a fool of myself.

Jerry spent hours pressing against me, touching my skin whenever possible while he showed me the strokes I needed to win. He would speak softly in my ear, giving me instructions for my next shot. I couldn't believe I could learn under these circumstances. All I wanted to do was kiss him and hold him close.

All sounds were muffled it was only Jerry and me in the room, according to us. By the time the night was over we had created a bond like no other. The energy in the room was exceptionally vibrant making like a force field around us. Everyone could see it, some were intrigued and others were flushed with jealousy.

Here I was a teenager living the life of an adult; not your everyday adult either. Someone who frequented bars and pubs, played pool, drank most men under the table all while flirting with all the boys (well men that is) to gain attention, or what I thought was the feeling of love.

Life was so free we made our own rules, and took everything for granted. "Why can't we have the knowledge learned in our later years cast upon those youthful days?" I wondered. I guess that would be too easy.

Back to the story at hand: Jerry and I. We spent most days and nights together. No one worked back then. If you didn't know how to work the system, there were many people eager to teach you. Free money they said, the government will send you checks every month and you don't have to pay it back. Almost unreal!

Before I learned of this system I did have a job. Now this is a pure example of how once you set your mind to something you have the power to make it happen. My brother and I had heard of a restaurant bar opening soon that was hiring. We decided to apply. It was okay for Mason as he was applying to be a busboy, a position that did not require experience nor age restrictions. However, the only position available for a young woman was waitress or bartender, or hostess, but that position didn't make much money. Wait a minute, the legal drinking age was nineteen at the time and I was only sixteen. Then there was the experience aspect of it. I thought for a moment and asked myself, "How can I make this happen, I really want this job." Then the ideas started flowing. I could just say I worked somewhere before. What if they call? I once read a statement from a book called You Were Born to Be Rich by Bob Proctor. This statement was not quoted by Bob, it was first shared with him by a man named Clarence Smithison. Since then Bob loved it so much that he has been sharing it with many people.

For countless hours each week of my life I would wonder why I was so different than so many others who had been through such tragic situations in their lives. Why did I continue to go forward no matter what? This was the statement Bob Proctor referred to that summed it up for me. One word really, "faith". The definition of faith he said is the ability to see the invisible and believe in the incredible and that is what enables believers to receive what the masses think is impossible.

This also reminded me of a poem a guy showed me years ago. He said he did not write it and did not know who did because it was signed anonymous. However, it always stood out in my mind and somehow I memorized it and still make reference to it today.

We the willing, led by the unknowing,

Are doing the impossible, for the ungrateful,

We have done so much, for so long, with so little,

We are now qualified, to do anything with nothing.

Kind of a crazy statement but it somehow it gave me the strength and belief system to tell myself I could do anything.

So in order to get the job as waitress I had to complete an application and give them previous work experience, which of course I could not possibly have, being underage. Well, if I gave them a place far away like long-distance maybe they wouldn't call. Immediately I remembered a bar I had some drinks in Vancouver, when I was with Bill. Okay, so that covers the experience part. I had already convinced myself that I could do the job. I had watched people serve me drinks and food for years while dining out. It couldn't be that hard, money and giving change would be easy too since

I had some experience working the flea markets with Mavis my stepmother, I thought. The only thing left was the age thing. What to do, what to do? I remembered I had my friend's identification in my purse because she loaned it to me when I was going to the bar one night to get in. I was a born leader especially with my friends, I knew if I called and asked her if I could use it for this job she would say yes. So, I did just that.

As I thought, my friend Crystal Stevens said yes. With all my information at hand my brother and I took the bus to Bobbi Jo's restaurant bar to apply. Lo and behold, within one week both of us got jobs. I was so excited, not only that but after three weeks working my boss came to me and said, "Crystal, I know a lot of people lied on their applications."

My heart started racing; I thought this was it, I had been caught. It didn't help that for weeks of working with my brother that he kept calling me Michele. People started asking, "Why do you keep calling Crystal, Michele?" He quickly lied and said that was my middle name.

No, that wasn't what my boss had to say. He said, "Crystal, I know you didn't lie in your application, I can tell by the way you know your work. I would like to make you my head waitress."

I almost collapsed with relief, then my chest rose; I raised my head to display a gleaming smile. As I knew now that I did it. If I wasn't sure before, that a person can do anything they set their mind to, I sure knew it now.

With Jerry and all my friends at the Edgewater bar every day having fun without me I just couldn't take it. I started calling in sick at Bobbi Jo's and eventually quit. I did feel bad because the boss kept asking my brother to tell his sister to come back, "I will hire her back." The power of the booze, drugs, and camaraderie won over in the end. Also, the fact that everyone told me how I could get money without working certainly helped matters as well.

The more time I spent with Jerry the better I got at pool, sometimes even beating the teacher. I could not resist playing every chance I could get. As I started playing for money and beers it got even more interesting. I could pretty much drink for free and leave the bar with more money than I went with.

The owners of the Edgewater, I can't remember their names right now, so let's call them Joseppe and Fabio. They looked like twins although I didn't believe they were. Both short, about five–foot-five inches, curly black hair puffed out in a circle around their head like an Afro, thick bushy eyebrows, large noses and thick lips, a couple of standard Portuguese guys. They always wore blue jeans and a dress shirt sometimes with a blazer over top.

Joseppe and Fabio were great; very easy to get along with. We had some clout there because we were regulars. It was almost like the mafia of its time. Now you would call us a gang in today's terms, there were leaders and followers. I was always the leader of the females and at the time Jerry was the leader of the men. There was a fair amount of responsibility that went with that. Not only did you have to control your group in various situations, you also had a number of other duties.

Before I get into that I want to explain how one got or obtained these leadership roles or positions. First you needed to be in the bar most of the time to hold your space.

Second, you needed to be tough, confident and outspoken

to keep your position. Many people who came through those doors were jealous and wanted the power we had.

At a moment's notice one needed to be prepared to defend their title if need be. So yes, I spent many days fist fighting or what they called it back then "pounding the shit out of people" week after week.

Now you couldn't be in power if you did not know how to play pool. This was another game of power that went on. As you continuously run table and win each game a quarter is placed on the side of the pool table as competitors try to win your title. Most times they would lose and sometimes there would be fights afterwards due to the sore losers and their pompous attitudes, but either way it was all fun. I would have to say that other than sex, winning at pool and fighting were second best.

As leader you needed to defend your crew or group, the followers. These were the people that weren't strong enough to stand up for themselves; the underdogs is another name. The followers loved watching you with your power and control. Their eyes watched you intently, as if in an adrenaline state. Their power comes from your power; you make them feel strong. As leader, if anyone speaks or looks at one of your crew the wrong way you are quickly there to defend.

On the business side of things the leader had to do all the negotiating with the bar owners. For example, someone has no money on hand but they have their welfare check and the bank is closed. The leader finds the solution and negotiates with the owner of the bar to cash the check as long as the person will spend 'x' amount of dollars in his establishment. The introductions are made by the leader and the transaction completed. Joseppe and Fabio would not do this for just anyone; they were relying on the leader's word that everything would go smoothly.

Also, if any fights broke out in the bar the person who did not belong to our group would be kicked out. No matter whose fault it was, we had the power since we were basically funding his establishment day in and day out. It's an unwritten rule that with favors came 'IOU's' or collections. The day had to come for me.

***

Joseppe and Fabio were hosting a bikini contest at the Edgewater to try to encourage newcomers. Anyone could sign up. I can't even remember what the prizes were; probably your picture in the paper and free drinks or two hundred dollars or something like that. Anyway, I was not going to do it. Everyone kept saying, "Ya, ya, you should sign up, you will win for sure."

All I kept thinking was how my team would respect me after I was prancing around half naked in a pub. It just didn't seem right. I was adamant I was not going to do it.

Then the night of the contest arrived. The bar was packed. The contest was being held downstairs away from the pool table. Joseppe told one of my friends to let me know that he needed to speak to me, it's important. So I went up to the bar and asked him, "What's up?"

He said, "I see you are not registered for the contest tonight."

"No," I replied, "definitely not."

He said with a very serious look on his face, "If you do not go in this contest I will personally bar you for life from coming back here."

I said, "You won't do that."

He begged and pleaded with me saying that his reputation was on the line; he wanted to make sure he had some nice looking girls in the contest and he felt I was one of them. After much pressure I agreed only if he would give me two free shots of tequila to get my nerve up. He agreed so I ran home and got my suit and came back for the contest.

My whole team was there sitting in one area. Jerry was around but did not seem to want to sit anywhere. Now that I think of it, he seemed almost nervous. There were six contestants, two in one-piece outfits and four in bikinis. It was hilarious; a couple of old broads like, what were they thinking? There was a middle-aged one with some kind of chain belt around her waist that looped down and around her lower belly to hide her enormous, deep stretch marks probably from having children. Then a very white-skinned blonde-haired slightly overweight girl about 20 years old. A girl named Madeline who I heard was a stripper and me.

I was in fairly good shape for my age and considering the amount of drugs and drinking I did. Now Madeline however, as I mentioned earlier, was a stripper; not very good looking in the face I thought, but she had a good body. She took her pop bottle glasses off to present herself in the contest. Now, remember, Jerry, was there pacing around like a wild animal stuck in a cage. At the time I couldn't quite figure out why he wouldn't sit at my table with me and my friends like usual. Through my curiosity I would soon find out why.

Overwhelmed with lots of alcohol and drugs in order to get

the nerve up to do this, I confidently pranced around the stage to show what I had. The crowd cheered as the emcee called out my number. Well that put me on an even better high than I was on before. It was my lifelong dream to be on stage. Throughout most of my life I would be reaching for that stage in one way or another. The bikini contest was just one of them.

So again the crowd cheered at the Edgewater Hotel to cast their vote out for the hottest chick there. After the elimination of most of the contestants there was only Madeline and myself left. Even if I didn't have the hottest body I had good looks in my face and a personality that everyone loved. In the end I came in first place and Madeline came in second. We both received trophies. In addition to that, my picture would appear in the Toronto Sun; pretty exciting.

***

My suspicions were increasing regarding Jerry, especially due to his unusual behavior that night. I just had to find out why. I went over to talk to him several times but he was very evasive in his responses to my questions. A few minutes later out of the corner of my eye I caught Jerry talking to Madeline. My face started burning with jealousy. Then I analyzed his body language a little more and suddenly it came to me; Jerry knew Madeline before that day. Now, I needed confirmation before I could plan my retaliation. Thinking quickly as soon as Jerry moved away from Madeline, I went over to her table pretending to congratulate her on her second place win and asking her to see what her trophy looked like. Then through the conversation I slipped in my investigative question nonchalantly. "How do you know Jerry?"

Madeline responded, "He is my boyfriend." My heart stopped and my breath seemed to dissipate for a moment while in shock. I was furious.

Now I was an upfront person, tell it like it is, whenever-the-urge-came-up-type of person. So I immediately said, "What a bastard." Madeline looked up at me in absolute astonishment not knowing why I would say this about her boyfriend and then she defiantly said, "Why would you say that?" I did not like secrets so I blatantly told Madeline that I had been dating Jerry for some time now. And that he had not mentioned that he had a girlfriend.

Now there were two really pissed off women who instantly had a connection. We talked and talked, revealing all the times when Jerry's absence could not be accounted for in each other's lives, taking every opportunity to meet eyes with Jerry around the room, each giving him a look of death. Jerry paced frantically, now realizing the jig was up. He could not approach either one of us to manipulate us with his lies. He just couldn't take it anymore and left.

Meanwhile, Madeline and I were formulating our plan of revenge. Madeline apparently lived with Jerry and said she wanted to move out. She was terrified to do it on her own because she said Jerry had beaten her before. I was shocked at hearing this because Jerry had not ever attempted such things on me. Matter of fact, I had put him in his place several times. For this reason and the fact that I loved to help out the underdog I offered to accompany Madeline with her move. As the plan continued to develop Madeline said, "Why don't you move in with me just in case he comes to my apartment?" We also decided this would be the ultimate payback. To add to the torture we decided not only to move in together but to move in the apartment across the hall. Well, there is nothing like a vindictive woman; never mind two of them.

So we put the plan into action. Madeline and I went to her place. Before going in to her apartment we went to speak with the superintendent to rent the apartment across the hall, which was empty. The superintendent agreed and gave us a key. Moments later we arrived at Jerry and Madeline's place. Upon opening the door Jerry was there drinking a beer trying to figure out what lies to tell Madeline. To his shock I followed behind Madeline into the apartment. Now he was really freaking out, caught red-handed. His face went red; he began pacing and then said, "What is going on?" Madeline confronted Jerry with his infidelity and notified him that she was moving out. As she started packing her things Jerry started yelling at her saying she was not taking anything with her. She shouted back at him calling him a fuckin' asshole and a no-good two-timing bastard. Which, I am sure she would not have been that forceful had she not known I was there to back her up.

Jerry was so angry hearing her say these things right up in his face that he forcefully pushed her down on the couch. He yelled loudly and viciously at her, threatening to punch her out. Well, that was it I couldn't take it anymore. I charged over to Jerry and pulled him back, grabbed him by the shirt and with all my strength and built-up anger I threw him across the room. With a deep, harsh powerful voice I said, "Sit the fuck down, and if you move I will kick the fuckin' shit right out of you." Jerry obeyed. Unlike Madeline, I was pretty vicious and Jerry had seen me fight before. Many times I pounded the shit out of guys' six-foot or more, relentlessly. Jerry knew not to mess with me. Madeline however, was so impressed; her fear of him immediately dissipated and her cocky attitude prevailed.

She packed all her things and moved them next door. Jerry said, "Don't worry, I know where you live. It is not over yet."

I said, "Oh really, well guess what? I am going to be living with Madeline so don't even think about any bull shit." His mouth dropped open in absolute shock; we were really drilling it into him.

When Madeline and I went into our new apartment we laughed and screamed with excitement. Nothing felt better to us right then than paybacks, the ultimate success. We celebrated our victory with some bottles of wine. Just outside our bedroom window was the roof where we camped out for days. We pulled an old mattress out onto the roof, plugged in a radio just inside the window and put on our bikinis and went tanning. All the while Jerry could see and hear us in his apartment that also led to the same roof patio.

We laughed and partied loudly while bashing Jerry as much as we could. We really were rubbing the dirt into his open wounds. Well of course this living situation could not last forever. Technically, we women were rivals, who only came together with a common purpose. Jerry knew he could manipulate Madeline and did so any chance he got. Madeline started to feel guilty and I could see that Madeline wanted to get back together with Jerry. As soon as I figured this out I knew I must separate myself from observing this inevitable reunion. I told Madeline that I would move out and since she was still hung on Jerry that she should just go back. Madeline had really wanted to say that but did not want to hurt my feelings. So after my announcement Madeline was relieved.

I did not move all of my things there anyway or give up my apartment. I must have known subconsciously that this setup would not be forever. Off I went back to my room at Mindy's mom's place.

As you know when something happens on the not-so-good side of things your emotions react by going through the various stages. First, one usually experiences anger. I experienced this full force up to the point of moving in with Madeline. However, now that I was back home and I knew Madeline and Jerry would soon be back together I started to feel sad and lonely. All kinds of thoughts ran through my mind. I had been used and lied to. My anger about men turned into self-destruction. My constant search for meaning made me believe this must be my fault again.

CHAPTER TEN

TO LIVE OR DIE

As I searched through my database of memories I found it was always me who was at fault, although now in my later years I realized that this was not so. Unfortunately, all the experiences stemming from my birth kept amplifying in my mind. This is a good example of the Law of Attraction in a negative way. The more I thought about all the horrible things that happened in my life the more I blamed myself. Again I was at a point of deep, deep depression. Feeling lonely, isolated and not worthy of life. No one would miss me if I died and certainly I would then be free of all the pain.

I decided it was time to end my life here on earth. This time it would work. I would not cut my wrists because I had tried that before unsuccessfully. Besides that was painful and I knew I could bear no more. I went to my mother's place knowing she would have some pills I could take. Believing that my mother really didn't love me since she had not cared enough to change her life and save her children from harms way while we were young. This being said I could just take them while I was there, go to sleep and not wake up.

When I arrived at my mother's house Meigan was of course wasted like she was most of the time. I asked her if I could have some of her pills to take. In her drunken state Meigan handed them to me. I grabbed a glass of water and proceeded to take a bunch of pills. In my mother's inebriated state she was still alert enough to know I was swallowing too many. She told me, "That's too many, ya will kill ya self," in her half-wasted Guyanese accent.

I defiantly said, "I don't care, I don't want to live." Then moments later I lay down in the bed prepared to die.

Even though my mother was not even fit to take care of me deep down inside she loved me; she loved all her children in fact. Meigan had her own pain and suffering to deal with, constant demons haunting her every breath, guilt and regrets without the strength or willpower to pull out of it. It was just too much pain. Within a few hours when she realized I was not waking up somehow she was able to pull strength hidden within her soul. She picked up the phone and called the police. Through her babbling, drunken words she told them her daughter had overdosed.

Several days later I awoke in a hospital bed. They had pumped my stomach trying to discharge as much of the pills as possible. The hospital had already called my father to say they did not think I would make it. And if I did I might be a vegetable. I lay there unable to move, catheter in and IV. I could see my father by my bedside crying and my sister was there too. Jenny tried to talk to me as soon as she saw my eyes open. I was completely paralyzed from the chlorpromazine nerve pills I had taken. Sounds echoed from my throat as I tried to speak. But my tongue would not move so I sounded like I was a baby just learning to talk. Aaaa Aaaa Aaaa. I felt like I was making sense in my own head and could not understand why no one was answering me. While my dad was crying my sister was laughing. Laughing so hard the tears poured down her face. Now, I know that sounds almost inhumane but it was a nervous laugh. Something that Jenny and I both had no control over in situations such as this. We once laughed at a funeral, again for the same reasons; just nervousness.

The angels saved me that night as there must've been some other purpose for my life. It was a cry for help! All along the way I wanted to be happy but my struggle seemed to be causing me more sadness. I could not trust people. Even the ones I thought were being fair and honest would hurt me in the end. The more I thought about it the more I realized true love would not come from men. Sex was just sex; it really meant nothing to me. It was love I needed. Who could I give love to that would give that same love back without question?

Grasping at straws I found my answer, a child. If I were to have a child he or she would love me unconditionally. I knew I could give that child all the things I did not have. Never let them feel unwanted or lost in this world. The more I thought about it the more I realized this was the best course of action. I didn't really want to die, not deep down inside anyway. When I thought about how I could accomplish this I knew I would need a man. The only man I knew at the time was Jerry; yes he was an asshole and totally unreliable. In this case these qualities were perfect since I really didn't want him anyway. All that was required was his sperm.

One night my friend and I called a meeting with Jerry. I explained to him that I wanted to have a baby without keeping the man. I told him I was looking for someone just like him who would not want the responsibility of the child in his life. I asked him if he could help me make a baby and promised I would not ever approach him for help regarding the child. I also notified him that I did not want him to have any part in the child's life. The idea was perfect for Jerry. He could get free sex with no ties, just like he wanted. And I would have the child I dreamed would heal me from my sorrows.

So now at eighteen years old I began having sex with Jerry with no protection. After a few tries I gave up on Jerry because I really couldn't stand him after what he did. I figured if it was meant to be whatever sex we had already would have worked. I continued to party not really thinking this idea was going to be successful anyway. A month passed and I missed my period and a light went on in my head maybe I'm pregnant. I quickly ran to the drugstore and purchased a pregnancy testing kit. Sure enough I was pregnant and went to the doctor's to confirm.

Only a child myself I really had no idea what I was in for. The doctors told me not to smoke or drink alcohol as it would cause harm to the baby growing inside me. But there was no trust in my mind of what people said, everyone lies or mistreats you, even the doctors. I remember when I was fourteen years old and went to see the doctor for a check-up. His name was Dr. Shalom, a Jewish doctor my mother had used for years. This was my first experience having an internal examination. What a horrible event, no doctor had ever touched me down there. To top it all off while he had his hand in their moving it around in my vagina he asked me if it felt good. My gut told me this was not something a doctor should be saying to a young girl, or anyone, for that matter. Since then my trust for doctors was shattered.

Men, they were all perverted. All they wanted from me was sex. My hate for men continued to escalate with each new experience. Brick by brick I began to build a wall around me, harboring anger in my soul. So when the doctor gave advice I felt in my heart that they were lying to me. They just wanted to ruin my fun. All I had left for my sanity was the partying I did with my friends. Although I continued to drink and smoke the amount had decreased simply because it did not make me feel good. My belly and breasts became larger and soon I would be wearing maternity clothes that one of my friends had given me. Blue jeans with an elastic front and a big balloon-shaped top. Much different to the maternity wear of today where the clothes are contoured to the shape of the belly, clearly exposing your condition.

I had an assumption that because I was pregnant men would somehow leave me alone. I was wrong because one day I was standing outside the store with my friends chatting. To my surprise and disgust a short fat man walked over and asked me if I wanted to go with him. He said he would pay me good money. I couldn't believe it, couldn't he see that I was pregnant and I told him this. He smiled, panting, saying, "Yes that's okay," almost excited like. How disgusting, I thought and told him to go fuck himself. A few minutes later we were walking home from the store and there he was. He was sitting in his car jerking off. What pigs they all are, I thought. When we got home we called the police on him.

***

As much as I told myself that I hated men I still felt lonely without them. One night my friends invited me to a party across the street. They said there would be a barbecue and some drinks. I could never miss a party even though I was about four months pregnant. It was there that I would meet and fall in love with Daniel. He was about five-foot-ten, slim build with strong arms built up from his carpet laying job that he had. He had nice blue-black hair, cut short and feathered back and wore glasses. Daniel was a country boy from a small town near Québec called Renfrew. He had a gentle kindness about him that I could not help being attracted to. Not to mention his sweet French accent, which came from his bilingual upbringing.

Daniel had recently broken up with his girlfriend who was his childhood sweetheart. The two of them came to Toronto about a year earlier to find work. Daniel got a job right away as a carpet layer and she got a job in an office as a secretary. She did not like Toronto and decided to go back to Renfrew. Because Daniel did not want to leave and they were fighting anyway they decided to split. Daniel found me very exciting as compared to his quiet shy hometown girl that he had dated for years. He knew I was pregnant and alone and he was willing to accept the whole package.

There was another couple who lived in the same building as Daniel, their names were Collette and Jason. Collette was a heavyset girl with long brown curly hair. And Jason was a tall mulatto man about six-foot-four and thin. They had been childhood sweethearts. The four of us became good friends over the months to come. Collette confided in me saying she feared for her life, that this relationship they had which seemed perfect to us outsiders was not so perfect. Me being the defender by nature wanted to protect her, I gave her guidance that she should leave him and not let him abuse her anymore. Easier said than done, this statement rang true for Collette. Collette convinced herself that Jason would change and continued living in his demise. I felt very strongly against this type of behavior from what I had gone through with my relationship with Bill. I could completely understand what Collette was going through.

Everything seemed to be going well for them for a while until one day it all changed. Daniel and I were just outside of the building on our way to his van to go out for a ride. Collette came stomping out of the building and Jason followed after her. They were arguing and swearing at each other while they walked. Collette came right over to me and quickly explained to me that he was hitting her inside and she was afraid for her life. I was her only friend and she knew I would protect her.

Jason came over and tried to grab Collette looking like he was ready to beat her. I immediately blocked him and said, "Come on, Jason; you and me, let's go. Try me, I will kick the fuck out of you." Even though I allowed the abuse from a man in my life before I did not put up with much from other men that I didn't love. I was crazy and had beaten men as big as Jason before, I had so much pent-up anger in me from all my years of life on the streets I had no fear. Jason backed down immediately; it was as if a light went on in his head.

His anger was not towards me it was for the woman he was supposed to love. He seemed to calm right down then turned around and went back into their apartment. Again I coached Collette about leaving him. I explained to her that she didn't deserve to be treated that way. Collette agreed it was time and that she had had enough.

One week later, January 28, 1985, Daniel and I heard sirens just outside the apartment. We quickly dressed and went out to see what was going on. There were many police cars and an ambulance in front of the building. They were wrapping yellow ribbons around the front of the building and would not let anyone pass. "Oh my God," I gasped. "I hope nothing has happened to Collette," I thought. The police wouldn't say anything but later that day the rumors came out that Jason had murdered Collette. News reports later confirmed these suspicions. I realized at that moment this could have been me. I had stood up to him just last week calling him on for a fight. This guy obviously was angry enough to kill. Somehow I was spared. My Angels and God kept me from harm's way. But poor Collette, she finally did listen to me and was about to leave him when it all came to an end. Although I originally felt I had given her the right guidance I now felt this unbearable guilt within me that maybe if I had kept my mouth shut then Collette would still be alive. This experience would definitely change the way I looked at my own personal relationships in the future.

This was the story in the newspaper:

Killer gives dying mate final kiss by Steve Payne

Jason Townsen stabbed his lover twice, then whispered "goodbye, I love you" as she lay dying in a bathtub, an Ontario Supreme Court judge was told yesterday.

Mr. Justice Frank Callaghan sentenced Townsen, 43, to life in prison for the "cold-blooded killing, " with no eligibility for parole for at least 12 years.

Townsen had pleaded guilty to second-degree murder in the January 28, 1985, stabbing of his common-law wife, Collette Townsen, 35, whom he had known since childhood.

Court heard that the woman told Townsen she was leaving him, but Townsen said he couldn't go on without her.

They discussed the matter into the early hours, had a short sleep and awoke at 7:30 am

"While she was in the washroom applying her makeup I went in and sat on the bathtub and caressed her and asked her not to leave," Townsen told police.

She again told him she was leaving.

"I got up, went to the closet, removed the survival knife and case from the closet... I walked towards the washroom," Townsen told police.

"She walked towards me and said, 'if you want to kill me, do it now. '"

Townsen said he held the blade to her abdomen.

"She said, 'if you're going to do it, then do it.'

"With my right hand, I thrust the knife to the hilt."

Townsen told police he partially withdrew the knife, twisted it and plunged it back into the woman. He then "guided" the dying woman to a bathtub, applied her lipstick to himself and then kissed her twice on the shoulder saying, "Goodbye, I love you." Townsen then "cleaned up" The King St., West apartment and went to a police station.

After this tragic ordeal I realized that when you think you are in control, you really are not, that the person who loves you could take your life away at any moment. At this point I was very happy to be with Daniel. He never hit me or got angry enough to even threaten me.

***

Two months after that incident my water broke when I was seven months pregnant. I did not even know what it was at the time. I called my sister crying saying I peed myself and it had soaked my pants. My sister Jenny knew right away that my water broke and told me to go to the hospital.

I called Daniel and he rushed me to the hospital. Fifteen hours later after much excruciating pain and an epidural at the last minute that did not have time to take effect, the baby was born. There she was a beautiful baby girl I named her Cassandra Lee Passion.

Cassandra was two months early so she was immediately put in an incubator. She had many wires hooked up to her and a tube inserted down her throat for feeding. She remained in ICU for several weeks and I would visit her each day. This was all so new to me, the nurses and doctors would look at me strangely when I came in because I was so young.

Prior to Cassandra's discharge the doctor met with me to tell me that because the baby was born too early that her lungs had not fully developed. And that Cassandra was having apnea spells where she would forget to breathe. They said it was mandatory for me to first go through training for baby CPR in case it happened at home. Also, I would need to get an apnea monitor that Cassandra could lie on in the crib. It was a mat that could sense her heartbeat and if it stopped an alarm would go off. That way I would wake up and go through the procedures to get her breathing again.

I was collecting welfare at the time and the rental of the machine would be a cost I could not afford. So I called up the welfare worker and they agreed to pay for it. Once Cassandra was healthy enough and the monitor in place she was released from hospital. This was so exciting for me to finally have someone to love me unconditionally and that I could love back.

For months I took Cassandra everywhere. People loved her. She had beautiful blue eyes just like Jerry. Jerry did see the baby but as agreed upon he did not want the responsibility of caring for her. It was Daniel who was known as her father. About three and a half months later the welfare worker called me and asked me, "How long will the baby need to be on the apnea monitor?" I did not know and told him I would check with the doctor. The welfare worker said, "Yes you should do that because it is costing us money."

So I made an appointment with my doctor and explained everything that the worker had said. The doctor examined Cassandra and said, "She seems to be okay, so you could probably take her off the monitor now." Within a week the welfare worker had made arrangements for the unit to be picked up.

When Cassandra was four months old, only a few weeks after the monitor was taken away, I woke up to a silence I had not heard before. My heart raced as I ran to the room where Cassandra was, knowing by this time she should already be awake crying to be fed. When I looked in the room and saw baby Cassandra lying there motionless and her head was a bluish color. I grabbed and shook her trying to wake her up.

Panic completely overwhelmed my body and all the training they had given me at the hospital was emptied from my mind. I ran with the baby in my arms screaming, "Help me, help me my baby isn't breathing." Tears poured down my face as I paced back and forth on the sidewalk. Screaming, "Please, please, somebody help my baby." Within minutes the fire department arrived first and took the baby from my hands. They tirelessly tried to revive her as I bawled profusely on the street.

Many people gathered and tried to comfort me but nothing seemed to work. Shortly after the police arrived in an ambulance, and the ambulance drivers rushed Cassandra to the hospital while the police drove me. Upon arrival at the hospital I was placed in a waiting room for what seemed like hours to me. I had no track of time. All I could think about was my baby, praying that she would be okay.

The door opened and three solemn looking people entered the room. All sounds around me dissipated except for the voice of the doctor. "I am sorry we could not save her." One of the people he brought in with him was a priest who wanted to comfort me and pray for me. I screamed out, "No! I want my baby; I can't lose my baby." Tears flowing down my face, my chest tightening, I felt as though I had died too at that moment. I paced the room feeling panicked and claustrophobic as if the walls were caving in on me.

I then realized the third person the doctor had brought in with him started approaching me as if to restrain me. I quickly realized this must be a psychiatrist thinking I was losing my mind. I feared he would lock me up or put me in a straitjacket. I knew I had to calm myself down in order for them to let me leave. The psychiatrist asked if I had family they could call. I quickly said, "Yes, I have my mother, she does not have a phone but I will go and see her right now."

Because I was relatively calm they allowed me to leave. I ran out of the hospital crying all the way to my mom's place. When I told my mom what had happened, my mother couldn't believe it. We cried together for hours before calling the rest of the family. I do not have much memory past that time other than having to go back to the hospital and identify the body with my sister.

Many people came to the funeral and even Jerry was in tears. I remembered taking Cassandra's baby koala bear that Daniel had won at a fair and placed it beside her in the coffin. I had no money for a funeral but my dad really stepped up to the plate and paid for everything.

After the funeral there was a get together at my house. This would be the last time I would see my mother and father in the same room. My dreams of them getting back together one day would be gone.

For weeks I cried and rocked a chair holding Cassandra's stuffed animals close in my hands. I would constantly hear a baby crying down the hall in Cassandra's old room. Many of my friends would come over and try to get me to snap out of my depression but to no avail. Lots of times I wouldn't answer the door or the phone. Finally I just couldn't take it anymore, unable to sleep, I grew weary.

Daniel finally was able to get me out of my place and had me move in with him. The months passed and things got a little easier. I partied doing drugs and drinking to help the pain go away. But each time I woke up I would feel sad. Christmas came closer and I was going to make a turkey for Daniel and myself. Daniel informed me a few days before that he would have to go back to Renfrew to visit his mother and he would be back Christmas Eve.

Once Daniel was in Renfrew he stopped answering his phone. I became very suspicious but hopeful he would still return and not leave me alone at Christmas. I bought a turkey and a case of beer plus a Christmas gift.

Christmas morning arrived and no Daniel. I continued to call him at his mother's; finally Daniel's brother answered the phone and said he was over at Melissa's next door. My mind raged with jealousy knowing this was his ex-girlfriend and suspecting he had gone back to her.

I was so overtaken by my sadness and now jealousy I again wanted just to die. It was the only way I could make it all go away. How could I kill myself this time, I thought? Cutting my wrists and taking pills did not work in the past. I had heard that people froze themselves to death with hypothermia. Since it was -20 outside maybe this would work.

As naïve as I was I put on my winter coat and headed down to the bridge. I had a lot to drink so my nerve was up. I crawled down under the bridge and huddled down. Not thinking that it would be better to go down there with no coat I sat down waiting to die. Hoping I would freeze to death. Hours passed and I had fallen to sleep. A chill went down my spine and shook me awake. I thought for a minute, did I die? As I glanced around my surroundings I quickly realized my plan had not worked. It was pretty uncomfortable for me under that bridge so I decided to go back to Daniel's apartment, turned off the heat, wrote a suicide note and lay there to die. Of course this did not work either as I woke up hours later freezing and sober.

Now the anger set in. How could he do that; just leave me there Christmas Day and let me buy a turkey and beer knowing I did not have much money. He could have been honest with me and said he might not be back. The more I thought about it the angrier I became.

Periodically I would go up to my Aunt Leslie's house to bar hop and party. My cousin Marissa would sometimes be there to hang out with. So I headed up there. Hoping I could convince my Aunt Leslie to allow Marissa to take a bus trip with me to Renfrew. Off I went and after several hours of convincing my aunt agreed to let her go up with me.

***

After a tireless journey on the bus to Renfrew we finally arrived at Daniel's mother's house. My heart was racing thinking about what might happen next. I knew Daniel would be shocked when he saw me at the door. Not only did I want answers, the truth, in fact, but I also wanted revenge.

Some young guy about sixteen answered the door. When I asked for Daniel he replied he was not there. So I left a message to tell him that I was here in town to see him and that if he knows what's good for him he will come and meet me at the hotel where we were staying. Within a half an hour of our visit while Marissa and I waited patiently at the hotel the phone rang. It was Daniel. I answered and as soon as I heard his voice I said, "You better get your fuckin' ass over here."

Daniel knew I had a cross side to me as he had seen me in many situations especially when I confronted Jason. He had no choice but to say yes. Marissa got a bit scared seeing this rage coming out of me. My face was beet red, my fists clenching as I paced around the hotel room. Marissa quietly asked, "What are you going to do when he gets here?"

I replied with, "I just want answers; I think I deserve at least that."

When Daniel arrived I could see that he was clearly a nervous wreck. His body trembled and his eyes wide opened. He also brought one of his older brothers with him, for protection I presume.

The silence in the air was so thick you could cut it with a knife as I glared at him with evil eyes. Finally Daniel broke the silence and asked, "Why did you come here?"

That was all I needed to completely explode. All the anger, hurt, and frustration lashed out at him like a cannon. I took him aside privately, which Daniel reluctantly agreed but knew his brother was not far if something happened. I then laid it all out on the table. "How dare you leave me all alone at Christmas? You said you would be returning so I bought a turkey and a case of beer for us to celebrate," I explained.

Daniel was very apologetic but that wasn't enough for me. I wanted answers; I wanted him to pay for my pain and suffering. With my teeth clenched together as I spoke, my fists clenched and my body leaning forward I scorned him. "You're nothing but a, two-timing mother fucker, you just used me and you should pay for your actions," I continued saying, "I have a good mind to not only punch the fuckin' shit out of you but also to go over to your other girlfriend's house and tell her all about you, what an asshole you are."

Daniel asked, "What do you want from me?"

"I want the truth," I said, "just the truth."

Daniel then went on with the whole story of how he and Melissa moved to Toronto for a job and to start a life there but Melissa did not like Toronto and after much discussion decided to return to Renfrew. Daniel wasn't sure at this point and since they weren't getting along let her go promising to return at a later date. But he said that both parties knew in their hearts it was over, until Christmas when all the memories came back as she lived next door to his parents. She pleaded with him to get back with her. And I guess the last time he saw her was a few months before after a fight with me when he went up for a visit. And now she just found out she was pregnant.

He proceeded to explain to me that I was just not the right person for him with all the violence and craziness that surrounded my life. He found me exciting, fun and great in bed but felt an obligation to his ex-girlfriend since she was the girl next door. He cried while telling me this saying he was scared and didn't know how to tell me. He pleaded with me to not hurt him or Melissa and that he would give me whatever I wanted. He also said how completely sorry he was for not handling things better.

On the outside I was extremely angry and mean but on the inside I truly did have a good heart. All I wanted was for someone to love me the way I knew I could give back. After hearing his story and seeing his pathetic begging and fearful state I felt I had caused him enough pain. I had my answers. Marissa and I returned home. It was a sad long ride with many tears. Again I felt like there was no one out there to love me. Daniel had given me money to pay for the unused turkey and enough to rent another apartment upon my return so that is what I did. So I was off to a new location and new adventures in my quest for love.

***

I found a nice one-bedroom apartment on Roncesvalles just up the street from the Edgewater hotel. I had become quite comfortable in the West End, I knew my only escape from all my pain and anguish would be partying and playing pool at the Edgewater with the friends I had met so far.

Day after day, night after night I continued to consume drugs and alcohol, whatever I could get to help me forget. My presence in the Edgewater was so frequent I felt like I ran the joint. I had made good friends with the bouncer, a big tall black guy named Wesley. He was a competitive bodybuilder and had won a few contests. Originally from Jamaica he had a strong accent, very tough on the outside but really he was a teddy bear inside. He didn't have any problems with me although I would get in fights with other patrons. Wesley knew I always had good reason and it also probably had a little something to do with Fabio and Joseppe, the owners, and my connection with them. They knew me and my friends were regulars and spent a lot of money in their bar.

One night I could not bear my sadness anymore. I tried to forget all the things that had happened to me in my life but nothing worked. When the pain became so prevalent I knew I could take no more. Once again I would consider taking my own life, ending these horrible memories of people who caused me pain.

While sitting with my group of friends who I really didn't think cared about me I announced my demise. I told them I was leaving and bid my goodbyes ending it with, "It was nice knowing you all," and left through the front doors.

As I exited the building the tears began to flow down my face in droves like a waterfall. Instead of heading left to go to my place I veered to the right towards the bridge. Every thought and painful memory repeated itself in my mind like a broken record. Finally ending with, "You're no good, nobody wants you, people just want to cause you pain," echoing in my head over and over again. It was as if I was in a tunnel and not only did the walls echo the empty mean words but the walls were caving in.

When I got to the bridge, I stood looking out over the highway deep below at the cars streaming by. No one cared about me, I thought, no one would ever miss me if I was gone. And maybe the pain would finally go away.

At that moment I had made my decision, my hands gripping tightly to the rails I eased over one leg, then the other. Still holding on waiting for the sign to let go and end my dreadful life to be crushed under the fast-moving vehicles below.

Not aware of any of my surroundings, just the noise in my head and the visions of peace I would have by ending my life this night. My hands opened slowly releasing me from the rails; my body began to lean towards the highway below, within seconds it would all be over. Then suddenly out of nowhere, a big strong hand grabbed me and pulled me back. It was Wesley, he must've seen I was depressed or talked to my friends and somehow thought to follow me.

With one quick jerk Wesley yanked me over the rails and back to safety. He asked, "What are you doing? You could have killed yourself."

I said, "I don't want to live anymore; it's too painful and no one loves me anyway. They won't care."

"How do you think I knew you were here? It was your

friends who told me something was wrong and to follow you," Wesley announced with discernment in his voice.

I could not really feel these words and still kept pulling towards the rails to jump. Wesley as strong as he was, just picked me up and put me in the car nearby and slammed the door to keep me in. But I had put my foot out to get out of the car at that time and the door slammed on my foot. That was like someone slapping a person in the face when they are freaking out to help snap them out of it. I could no longer remember why I was there. All I could think about was my sore foot and wanting to go to sleep. Everything else from that point was a blank.

The next morning I woke up on the front lawn of Mindy's house. I guess no one knew where my new place was and Mindy happened to be at the bar that night, when they asked, "Where can we take her to be safe," Mindy replied at her house. In my completely wasted state I refused to go in and just lay on the grass and said I will just sleep here.

Upon awakening several hours later I found myself lying on the grass in front of Mindy's house. My foot was paining me so bad and I had absolutely no recollection as to why I was in this state. Since I recognized it was Mindy's place I figured she might have some answers for me. I limped on one leg to the front door and knocked several times until Mindy answered. Mindy invited me in and explained that night's affairs.

I could not believe what I heard, and again realized that my life had once again been spared. That God with the help of my guardian angels must have had a better plan for me. The fact that I did not remember any of this made me afraid. I knew I would have to change this wild and crazy life of mine in order to survive. Although I had no idea at the time of how I would do this, I wasn't quite ready to give up all my partying but I could ease up on the things that caused me to black out. One thing I knew for sure was that straight liquor like tequila shots had to go. I made a pact with myself to be more careful with hard liquor and drugs.

I made my way back home and had a nap. That evening I awoke, showered and freshened up to head down to the Edgewater to shoot some pool. When I arrived the bouncer approached me asking if I was all right. I was so grateful for my life and thanked Wesley for saving me. All night long I was approached by all my friends with concern. They looked up to me because to them I feared nothing. Little did they know that deep within me was an inner sadness and pain that I could not escape from.

CHAPTER ELEVEN

IS THERE LIGHT IN THE DARKNESS

Several weeks passed and I became emotionally weak again. It was not easy for me to hold onto it so tightly, being strong all the time. Again the loneliness and sadness began to peek out. The last person to victimize me would soon appear. Dark auburn hair about shoulder length, tall, muscular man, about six-foot-two, with fair skin covered with a small amount of freckles. He was extremely good looking, with a sexy devilish smile, and bedroom eyes that glared at you with such depth. He was walking straight up to the pool table I was playing on. He placed a quarter down on the side making a loud clicking noise to ensure I noticed him. Of course I looked up and our eyes met only for a brief moment. I knew I was doomed. The energy that swarmed the room that moment took my breath away.

I kept my composure expressing my "you don't shake me attitude" and gave it right back to him. This strange new creature returned to his table, sat down, slouched back in his chair, legs spread apart displaying his package with one leg pointing forward as if to say, I'm in charge. His eyes never strayed from the sight of me as if he was trying to swallow me up from a distance. I could feel his eyes on me and would catch a glance out of the corner of my eye from time to time. I kept my cool, took a deep breath, raised my head slightly, sort of snobbish like and ran table on the guy I was playing pool with.

One ball after another, confidently showing this man who was watching me not to mess with me, that I would eat him alive, as the saying goes. Eight balls in a row, bang, bang, bang. Last shot, the eight ball, I called it one bank in the corner. Now if you don't know that much about playing pool I should let you know that bank shots are pretty difficult. Only the best of the best can make them. Within seconds I shot the white ball and hit the eight off the bank and rebounded it into the corner. "Yes!" I said out loud, bringing my fist from the air tight up to my side as if I was flexing my biceps. I hollered out, "I will have a Coors light," since I won, the loser must buy me a beer.

After taking a sip of beer and a drag of a cigarette I waited for the new stranger to approach. He remained silent and still continuing to strip me down with his eyes from afar awaiting direction. I looked down at the table to see only one quarter sitting and yelled out, "Who's next? As if I didn't know already. Underneath my tough exterior I was both excited and nervous at the same time thinking about this mysterious man.

Out of the corner of my eye I could see that he took the last sip of his beer and placed the bottle on the table, almost in slow motion. Not wanting to look too eager he rose up and did a slow walk over to me, each step he took toward the table my heart raced an extra beat. As he slowly approached he glanced quickly at the table to ensure there was only one quarter left standing there so as to ensure it was his turn, as if he didn't already know.

I took a deep breath as he approached the three feet mark and raised my head high to display my confidence even though I was trembling inside with a plethora of emotions. I looked way up at him with his tall lean stature as if I just noticed him approaching and said, "Are you up?" He knew I was playing coy with him and decided to play along. With a shy grin he raised his long arm and massive hand towards me to shake my hand and introduced himself as Roger. His strong hand completely covered mine but had a somewhat gentleness to the shake, just enough to show his softer, sexier side. Our eyes locked powerfully as we shook hands while I announced who I was. With all my inner strength and confidence I said, "Hi, I am Michele," maintaining my composure and keeping everything strictly professional. I treated him as if he was just another player although I felt otherwise. With a soft, sexy voice this intriguing man said, "I think I am up next."

Since Roger was new to the Edgewater I felt I should lay down the rules of the house. "Call shots only," I said, letting him know the level of seriousness within the game.

Roger responded with, "Of course," in his deep sexy voice.

I courteously asked, "What do you want to play for?"

Roger, seizing this open-ended opportunity moved closer and with a soft sullen voice said, "If I win you will come on a date with me."

My cheeks became flushed and my shyness came over me as Roger stared deep into my eyes. He continued by saying, "And if you win, you can have whatever you want."

As I was simply melting I remembered all I had been through with men and thought this is just another one in a different shell. Immediately a wall came up around me, giving me enough time to regain my composure. "Dream on," I responded, putting him in his place and completing my statement with, "We will play for drinks." Even though I completely had the hots for this guy I thought it best to play it cool.

Roger was even more intrigued with this tough chick controlling the pool table and decided he would play along. First game I won hands down, the whole time Roger watched me. He was more focused on me than the game. I continued to play coy while trying desperately not to let him in. I knew if I was to allow this to happen I could very well be hurt again. This battle in my mind continued throughout the next few games. At times, Roger would say some things so sweetly that it would pierce through my wall of protection and enter close to my broken heart.

We continued to play for beers while Roger pleaded for personal rewards instead. The subtle sexual innuendos were flying about all through the night from both parties. I quite enjoyed this game of teasing, knowing full well in my heart that I could have given in the first moment I saw him. But what fun would that be? This way I could get to know him a little and find out what he was all about.

Roger won the odd game in between and was feeling confident. He was flirting furiously in between shots, standing just outside the corner pocket so my eyes could see his strong physique ahead as I was ready to shoot the ball. I would do the same, standing powerfully holding my cue on the sidelines.

When my friends would come over to periodically chat, Roger listened intently at the conversation trying to find out what buttons he could push next. The more he knew about me, the stronger he played the game; the game of love and lust that is. He needed an angle to get even closer to me. Reading from my conversations with others he understood I was a solid person, and if you were on my side I'd back you all the way.

How could he do this, he thought? He had to think quickly because another guy had put his quarter on the table to indicate that he was up next. At any moment now our game would be over and his chances would be lost. He knew if I won that this new guy would be my main focus and he would have to get away from the table and give up his turn. And if he won I could leave the bar completely. This would not be good.

Roger was smart and devious and searched his brain for a plan. Last shot I sunk the eight ball creatively, two banks in the side--nothing could stop me now. All this admiring that Roger had been giving me gave me strength to continue to beat him down. When the shot was over Roger shook my hand and said good game.

Within seconds the new man arrived to claim his spot, followed by his friend who would sit on the sidelines and watch. As the guy picked up his quarter he must've sensed the bond that had developed over the past few hours with Roger and I and he asked, "Do you want to play partners?"

Roger turned to me, his eyes lit up and said, "We can beat these guys; let's show them what we can do."

After observing Roger's billiards skills for the past few hours I knew he was good. Only reason he didn't beat me was purely the distraction of his infatuation with me. I quickly agreed nonchalantly as if it was no big deal, now it was time to kick ass, I thought. I myself knew I was not playing to my full potential with Roger for the same reasons as him. But now we were a team, so lookout. I was relieved that Roger was still by my side. I was also intrigued by him and certainly did not want him to go away.

There is where it all began, as partners the two of us rocked. We were completely unstoppable; absolutely no one could touch us. The more we won, the closer we became, giving high fives, screams, and even some hugs. Any opportunity we had to be close to each other we took it. The first night we spent together we lay there talking, all guards were down, no one around to require us to raise a false front as we would so often do in public. It was amazingly powerful. We talked and talked about everything under the sun, mostly who we were inside and out and why we had come to be this way. We were blatantly honest with each other, sharing secrets that had been locked away. There were so many similarities amongst us that our bond grew stronger. Someone finally understood who each of us were, we thought.

After that night Roger and I spent as much time together as we could, each time even more powerful than the last. We exposed our innermost fears to each other, connecting in a way we never thought possible. True love; deep, deep true love arose out of our dark sides.

Roger had told me that he was part native; his mother was half and his father was full native. He said he had no papers to prove it because his father got drunk and sold their rights, which could be done in those days. I remembered him saying that he had a brother and a couple of sisters although I only briefly met the brother and one sister. Both of them looked much more native than Roger. He said they were from the Mohawk tribe and that his auburn hair, fair skin and freckles were common amongst Mohawks.

Roger explained to me that his father was abusive and had beaten and sexually abused him and his brother. His brother seemed to take it much harder simply by drinking excessively throughout his life. I only met Roger's brother once and he was pretty wasted. He looked very native in his features. Across his forehead was a deep scar almost as if it went down to his skull because his head was shaped funny from it. Roger explained that his father had hit him in the head with an axe. Brutal. I couldn't imagine one of my family members doing that to me; least of all my father.

Roger also explained that he had been in prison and had changed his life. Of course all of the reasons he was there he said were not his fault. He seemed so sincere and honest that I wanted to give him the benefit of the doubt and believe him. I was also still quite naïve to many things in the world. At this point in my life I never watched the news as it only depressed me. I felt life was depressing enough; no need to add to it.

Roger's mom and dad separated in later years, long after the damage was done. The one sister I met of Roger's seemed to have her life together. She had a good job and she owned a nice place downtown. The other sister was married and rarely ever talked to Roger. I had met Roger's mom who genuinely displayed her kind heart amongst a tough abused exterior. This was Roger's story, according to Roger, for now anyway. Bits and pieces would trickle out later, as all secrets do eventually come out.

***

Roger and I continued on with one of the most powerful relationships you could ever imagine. A very rare combination of two independent leadership roles combined into one. I had learned to stand up for myself over the years and Roger had the same traits but quadrupled from his stint in jail. It was me and Roger against the world. We would prance about flirtatiously with the opposite sex and then meet together to flaunt our commitment to each other. It was as if we would be saying to others, "You want me, don't you? You know I am good, don't you, and you will never be the same once you have me." Then the moment the fish was hooked we would act as though you can't have me anyway, and return to our stations together.

We were the leaders of our crew and no one would mess with us, even if they thought they could. We laughed, we played and we argued all the while testing the waters with each other. How far could we push each other before someone broke? I really loved Roger, he was not only tall, dark, and handsome but he was strong and could take care of me if I needed it.

Although we both displayed an enormous tough exterior each one knew the other's soft side. When alone, we would talk baby talk. "Wodge I wuv you," I would say. And Roger would respond with, "I wuv you too, sellers." If only people knew what went on behind closed doors. Our incredible lovemaking sessions would blow the lights out on a porno film and completely shock the nation. We experienced everything you could imagine. When we shared stories of our pain we spoke of God and how he saved us. We could party like no other and both of us left standing while others had crashed. But get on our bad side and look out.

This was how it went for the first while. I really believed in Roger and all he stood for. I laid my heart completely on the line wanting so badly to have someone to love me. Even though I was the leader amongst my crew, with Roger I soon became the follower. Roger knew the mind games like no other, and although I exhibited a false front I was extremely insecure. I truly did not believe I was worthy of much. The drugs and drinking helped give me the confidence to make people believe otherwise, except for Roger. All the while he was pouring his heart out to me day after day; his mastermind of manipulation was hard at work.

Each time we would get in an argument Roger would convince me that it was my fault. He would shoot out words of accusation and reasons why he was angry and blame me. As I became confused, not able to find answers as to why I behaved the way I did, the only conclusion was that it was my fault. Remembering my childhood and being a bad girl, feeling it must be me.

As the months passed, the arguments got worse and ultimately resulted in Roger hitting me. My automatic instinct was to fight for my freedom for my self-worth. I had promised myself after Bill that I would not allow this to happen again with anyone. But the more Roger apologized saying he would never do it again and if I hadn't done the things I did he would not have felt the need to hit me, the more I believed him. I knew I would be alone again in this world with no one to love me. Roger, the mastermind, knew this and preyed upon my insecurities. Coming up with all kinds of reasons why he had to hit me. All of it was because of what he said I did.

Now with a black eye I was convinced I deserved to be hit. I was just not a nice person and that is why all these things have happened to me in my life. Roger promised, "He would never hit me again;" hmmm, the famous line of an abuser. I convinced myself that since I deserved it anyway and Roger's apologies and promises were sincere that I would not leave him.

A little while would pass where all was glorious. True love stood strong and there was nothing that could stand between us. We were a match in so many ways, hovering on top of the world. However, with each new incident that occurred things got worse. Many times I feared for my life but I remained, feeling this was my fate and that I deserved it all, the whole time my self-confidence slowly being destroyed.

We were always trying various tactics to get enough money to party for the next week. I would sometimes ask my mom for money or pills that I could sell. Roger would work the odd job here and there in addition to obtaining some items to sell like stereos and jewelry. He would always say someone gave it to him or he found it in the garbage somewhere. I believed him, not giving it much thought at the time. Now looking back I realized they were probably all stolen. This type of thing sufficed for a little while, however our combined drug use was increasing. We needed a much larger source of income.

***

Roger got a job as a bouncer at a strip club. While he was there he came up with an idea for me. He suggested that I become a stripper and that I would make huge money. I immediately said no at first, "I can't take my clothes off for strangers like that." But Roger kept making me feel guilty like I was not contributing enough money to the relationship and that he was doing his part. On and on he went with every guilt trip he could find. He then said they were expecting me, and that he had already signed me up. I was sick to my stomach at the thought of it. Roger wouldn't let up. I could see the anger in his eyes when I continued to refuse. It was like his blood began to boil from his body up to his eyes and he finally laid the law down telling me I was doing it. He let me know he would provide as much drugs as I needed to get my nerve up, and that he did.

I smoked all kinds of hashish and drank straight shots of tequila and soon my mind was in a cloudy state, totally inebriated. So here I was with my burlesque entertainers' license, some skimpy clothes and a tiny little G-string, which was the only thing I was allowed to keep on. In later years that changed to completely naked but not yet, thank God. So I did what I had to do and danced and drank all night. By the second night Roger said, "You are drinking up all our profits, you need to not drink so much or you will be paying them to work."

By the third night I could not take it anymore. I told Roger I didn't like this and wanted to quit. He got very angry and threatened to punch me out if I did not show up for work. He was worried the boss would be upset with him because he pulled some strings to get me in. He then said he would lose his job because of me. He poured on the guilt with every threat and story he could come up with.

Roger had punched me close-fisted many times since his first promise never to hit me again. For this reason I feared for my life, especially when I saw the anger in his eyes. I really hated taking my clothes off in public. I begged and pleaded with Roger to let me quit but he refused. On the fourth night something happened between Roger and the owner. An argument about how many shifts I would do. The more shifts the more money, you see. Whatever happened I really didn't care, all I knew was that the many prayers I sent out to God pleading for my escape from this horrible, degrading job would be over. Roger came over to me just before my set and said, "We are leaving; get your things." I couldn't pack my things fast enough and did not even question. When the two of us got outside all I wanted to know was that I would never have to go back and this Roger confirmed.

I prayed in my mind all the way home thanking God for freeing me from this distasteful experience. But was I free? For months following I did not enjoy sex. Somehow I felt dirty, I tried tirelessly to forget those four days in my life, but Roger would not let me forget it so quickly. He used it against me in arguments to put me down saying things like you enjoyed it, you liked flaunting yourself about naked. Just the way he said it made me feel cheap and worthless, again another tactic to keep me in his control. I continued to do as much drugs as I could with hopes to forget that horrible experience in my life.

***

One night Roger and I partied at a club up the road from where we lived. Not my normal stomping grounds. Looking back I believe this was another way to control me by bringing me to places where I didn't know anyone. However, I couldn't change who I was, I liked talking to people. Roger became jealous and started arguing and threatening me in the bar. Up to this point, Roger had not abused me in public, so I was quite confident he wouldn't hit me while in the bar or on the street.

Suddenly Roger seemed to calm down, accepting defeat in the argument and he said let's go to another place. When we got just outside the door where no one could see, he grabbed me by the scruff of my shirt, threw me up against the wall and started punching me. I screamed and wiggled away, running frantically down the street as Roger chased me. I was terrified for my life. I could see people on the street walking and staring but no one was helping. They could see him chasing me while I was screaming, "Help me, help me!" But nothing, not one person stopped to help except a cab driver wanting a fare. I quickly jumped in the cab and pleaded with him to drive me quickly to my house. I ran inside and locked all the doors. Hours passed with no sign of Roger so I fell sound asleep, while my roommate lay sleeping on the couch.

By morning Roger had been drinking all night and stewing on the previous night's incident. He knocked on the door and before I could tell my friend not to answer she opened it. He pretended to be calm and said, "We need to talk, Michele." And he asked my friend if she could leave us alone and go out somewhere for now. We sat in the kitchen and began talking, Roger remained calm but I saw that dreadful look in his eye. Roger began his normal plan of manipulation, blaming me for the incident, cutting me up and making me feel like I deserved it. Although my self-worth was pretty much shot at this point I still had some fight left in me. I was fed up of being abused. Roger took a butcher knife out of the kitchen drawer and while holding it, twirling it around, his teeth clenched, and with a quiet eerie voice he said, "I could kill you with this, you know."

My heart raced but I tried not to show my fear. Roger grabbed me by the hair at the back of my neck and held the knife to my throat. He glared deeply into my eyes as if he could see right through me. His teeth exposed surrounded by his powerful jaw pulsating he leaned forward with these words, "I could just slit your throat right here." Now I had had enough, fed up of living in fear and feeling like I would die at any moment. In that split second I said, "Go ahead, why don't you just kill me and get it over with, I have had enough." Remembering back to Collette and Jason this statement could really have backfired for me. What was I thinking?

Lucky for me, for some reason, that statement snapped Roger out of his state. He released my neck and slowly brought the knife down and placed it on the counter. Suddenly, that soft side of him came flowing out, pleading for forgiveness. He cried big tears saying he was all messed up and needed help. That he loved me more than anything and did not want to hurt me. He promised to get help for his anger and said, "I will never hurt you again." I had heard this statement many times before but I had been beaten down so many times both physically and mentally that my self-worth was shot. I really did love Roger, the good side of him anyway. I also harbored a strong belief within that people could change. My need to help the underdog took precedence in my being. With all these things in mind I agreed to give it another chance vowing never to let him do this again to me.

Yet only days later another incident occurred and Roger started at me verbally. I snapped this time and bent over and picked up a solid oak coffee table with glass top and with a strength I did not know I had, threw it at Roger. I glared at him with deathful eyes and said, "Get the fuck out." Roger ran out the door so quickly, thinking I had gone mad. I was quite proud of myself standing up to Roger like that. Very pleased with the results I later that night locked the doors and went to bed forgetting all about the windows. Since we were on the second floor I felt I would be okay and fell fast asleep. My roommate was out for the night staying at another friend's place so I was alone.

In the wee hours of the morning I could sense eyes on me. Knowing how my gut generally was right I slowly opened my eyes just to check. To my surprise and shock, there was Roger about three inches from my face, his big strong hands approaching my neck. His eyes glossy and spaced out glaring at me. At that moment my heart raced and jumped into my throat, freezing my vocal chords. I tried to scream but nothing came out. With his eerie deep voice Roger said, "You thought you got me hey, I could fuckin' kill you right now and nobody would know, you'd be dead before anyone heard you."

As my life flashed before my eyes I thought this is it; I had now pushed him too far. Within that instant I faced the "fight or flight" decision and quickly rolled away to the opposite side of the bed, jumping up. He continued to threaten me while blocking the door. I knew the only way out was through that door. I bolted for it hoping to put him off balance so I could escape. Roger grabbed me and began punching me in the face repeatedly, holding my throat as I frantically tried to wiggle myself free. In my mind I pleaded with God to save me, to not let me die. Out loud I shouted out apologies to Roger to forgive me, that I was wrong. When Roger saw the blood pouring out from my face and maybe God's influence took over his soul, he stopped. Suddenly the rage inside him dissipated. A softening of his face prevailed and he realized what he had done. But it was too late. He had done what he promised never to do again. Imagine that?

Roger released his grip on me and guided me to sit down while he ran to get a cloth and ice to attend to my face. I sat on the couch almost lifeless, physically and emotionally exhausted. I had no strength left to fight back or escape. While Roger tended to my wounds like a devoted doctor, he pleaded for my forgiveness, each time slipping his words of wisdom as to why this happened. Most of it due to me he would say, even the parts where he was responsible he'd tell me that I knew what he was like and if I had not aggravated him this would not have happened. The more he manipulated my mind the more I believed I deserved it, it was a vicious circle. I was a terrible person and it was God's way of punishing me for the life I led. Yes, continuing on with this ludicrous relationship while believing this is my fate.

***

One night Roger and I decided to go to the Edgewater for some beer and pool. After entering, finding a seat and securing the pool table, Roger became edgy. His eyes stared into the distance, glaring dartingly as if they were lasers penetrating through metal. I could feel the enormous tension in the air. It was so strong it felt as though I was being strangled. I looked over to see what Roger was staring at and the only person I could see was the new bouncer that had started a few months back. I had met him and became somewhat friends of course to secure my authority in my bar and gain protection if needed.

He was a well-built bodybuilder type and I always liked working out but did not have a gym membership for a while. Mark, let's call him, had some weights at his house and offered to train me and get me on a vitamin regimen. So whenever Roger was off doing whatever I would meet at

Mark's place for a lesson. This was the first time Roger had seen Mark because he would normally want to party in other places.

Nothing was said but their eyes told everything. When I asked Roger what was going on he quickly disregarded his behavior and said everything is okay. I knew otherwise and planned to question him later. And that I did. One night while Roger and I were lying in bed chatting and being very open and honest with each other, I slipped in the question about Mark. Roger claimed that the two of them knew each other in prison. They were not friendly but knew who each other was. Apparently both of them planned to escape on the same day and Roger got away and Mark got caught. Roger said after that Mark labeled him a rat (tattletale) or pigeon and for this reason they hated each other. Roger having adopted these labels had to be put in solitary confinement, which meant he was in twenty-three-and-a-half hour of lockup per day.

Now Mark's side of the story was much different. He said that Roger was a woman beater and that he was extremely disliked amongst the inmates. I was naïve at the time and wanted to believe I was the only one who had been hit, that it was accidental and his first incidents of such so I accepted Roger's version of the story.

A few nights later while Roger and I were in the Edgewater playing pool and drinking, a fight broke out. Both Roger and I were absolutely wasted, popping Tylenol threes and drinking. I was so wasted I can't even remember what caused it, all I knew was Roger was involved. More than likely I had a few words to put into it, as well as his comrade. Mark, since he was the bouncer, threw me and Roger out of the bar, barring us from ever coming back.

Roger was pissed mostly from previous anger he had been holding on to regarding Mark but also due to this incident. I loved Roger and looked up to him. He was ten years older than me and so much wiser than me I thought. I fed off his every move especially his anger that night.

The two of us went back to my apartment to stew over the incident. Repeatedly reviewing everything that had happened over and over again, until we couldn't take it anymore and were about to explode. Roger while ranting and raving secretly was devising a plan in his mind. When it got closer to closing time at the bar Roger revealed his plan to me and walked over to the kitchen drawer and pulled out two knives. One butcher knife for himself and a smaller knife for me, which was all we had in the drawer. He ordered me to go with him to Mark's house.

At this point I was blacking in and out from all the drugs and drinking. I knew I must follow or Roger's rage could turn onto me. When we arrived at Mark's house Mark was not home yet and his girlfriend answered the door. Roger pushed his way in and I followed behind. He yelled out, "Where is he?"

Absolutely terrified, the young girl, tears in her eyes, voice shaky asked, "Who?"

"Mark," Roger said.

"He is still at work," she replied.

Roger then made her sit down in the kitchen threatening to kill her with the knife if she moved. Roger was very sketchy, pacing about all over the place. He ordered me to stand guard over the girl while he looked out the window for Mark's return. Even though I was wasted I didn't feel good about this. Paranoia was setting in. Roger decided he would watch over the girl, continuing to threaten her. My heart was racing and I decided to go look out the window. All of a sudden I saw a big huge guy coming down the street and four other guys with him. I reported this to Roger and told him we should go. "There are too many of them--we will be killed."

Whether I was hallucinating or not I really did not know, but I pleaded with him to leave all the same. Finally my persistence paid off and Roger agreed. After instructing the girl to stay put or we'd be back to get her, especially if she called the police the two of us ran out the door and down the fire escape.

By the time we got halfway home the police pulled us over and arrested us. We had knives in our possession and a witness to say what had happened. We were doomed. Face down leaning on the police cruiser Roger whispered to me these words, "If they ask you if I am married, just say yes. I will explain later." So here we were handcuffed in the back of a cruiser and I find out that the man I love and care about is married. I wanted to punch the shit out of him right then and there but couldn't because my hands were tied behind my back. Roger continued the conversation in the car saying he had been separated for quite some time and didn't love her. He also instructed me not to answer any questions when I got to the station.

Once we arrived at the police station we were placed in separate holding rooms, side-by-side. After what seemed like hours but was probably only minutes I heard big heavy footsteps approaching down the hall and a door open. It wasn't mine so I listened carefully to see if it was Roger's. I could hear voices but could not figure out what they were saying. Then I heard banging and punching noises as if someone was fighting or being beaten up. It must be Roger, I thought. Then the noise stopped and I heard a door open and shut at that moment I heard Roger yelling out, "Tell them about your dad, tell them about your dad." Then the door opened and two very large men dressed in street clothes and construction boots walked in. "What about your dad?" they said.

With all my past issues with the police I never once used my dad as a scapegoat. I wanted to be tough and accepted as part of the gang, not weak like a baby using my daddy to get me out of trouble so I never mentioned him before. Since Roger was the one I looked up to and was the reason I was there he must have a plan. So I followed his direction. When the man asked me a second time I said, "My father is a cop."

"Ya right!" they said doubtfully. "Where?"

So I told them where. At that moment the two men said they would be right back and left the room, never to return. A few minutes later two new men came in dressed in uniforms and very politely said, "Are you hungry ma'am?" Would you like something to drink?" The one good thing Roger did for me that night. He saved me from the beating I was to receive in the interrogation room. You see, all cops take care of their own, it is an unwritten rule. They are probably one of the biggest gangs out there when you think of it. So if you are caught doing something wrong or you are a relative of a cop, they will protect you as much as they can in support of their fellow officers.

I did end up with some charges that night but once they got to court they recognized that Roger with a record as long as his arm was the ringleader and main influence in this happening, ultimately pursuing him more with this incident.

I was released and Roger remained in custody and a hearing would be held on Monday to post bail. Because I believed what Roger said about not being with his wife I decided to try to get him bail money. I did not have any myself but there was a guy who worked at a car lot nearby my house, he often would help people out in the area. The story is that he used to be in trouble himself and someone helped him out so he wanted to give back. I approached him with my story and he agreed to put up ten thousand dollars surety for bail if Roger needed it.

***

Monday morning came and I was off to the courthouse. I was so proud that I was able to come up with the bail money for Roger. He would be so happy and surprised with my accomplishments. As I was walking down the hall towards the courtroom I saw a woman screaming, "You fuckin bitch, how dare you."

She was coming right at me. I looked behind me thinking she must be going towards someone else because I had no recollection of who this woman was. Then I realized that I was the only one in the hall. The woman was right up in my face saying, "How can you sleep with my husband, how do you think our daughter will feel when she finds out?"

"Daughter!" I shouted shockingly. "I didn't know he had a daughter, matter of fact I didn't know he had a wife until recently."

After everything calmed down a bit the two of us went and

sat down to talk. The woman whose name was Mia was Roger's wife. She produced a letter he had just written to her while in jail saying his story of what had happened. Telling her how much he loved her and their daughter and that I was just a fling. Up to this point I did not want to believe anything this woman was saying. However, the letter was clearly in Roger's handwriting and indicated the most recent events which only he would know, and to top it all off it was signed by him.

I was deeply in shock. Up until a few days ago I thought Roger was mine and mine only. I felt bad for this woman and her child. Not only that but how could this man betray me like this. Even though I spoke to Mia and saw the letter I still wanted confirmation. Confirmation from the man I loved as to the truth of this evidence. So I decided to go into the courtroom. I had already told Roger's attorney that I had ten thousand dollars surety bail to put up for him. Mia sat on one side of the courtroom and I sat on the other.

The announcement was made, "All rise," as the judge entered the room. A couple of inmates were called one by one before Roger. Each time I was desperately looking out for Roger to enter. All I could think of is, there must be an explanation, he would not do this to me, he loved me. Then the door opened and in came Roger handcuffed and shackled and all black and blue.

The Crown prosecutor presented his case first, listing out the new charges and all the previous convictions. I was shocked when I heard all this because Roger had only told me about one thing. Where did this list come from? Maybe Mia was right. She did show me the huge scar on her forehead and said Roger had beaten her after throwing a plate of spaghetti at her head and splitting it open. She said,

"I was given about one hundred stitches to seal it up."

As I listened to the prosecutor and then the defense lawyer I stared at Roger trying to make sense of all of this. Then in absolute disgust, I saw him look to one side and wink at Mia with the one eye closest to her. To top that off he had the nerve to then turn towards me and wink at me with the other eye. That was it, the last straw. I had enough of his shit.

Just then his lawyer announced that he had bail money from his wife of ten thousand dollars and another ten thousand dollars surety from the car lot guy that I had brought. At that moment I stood up and said, "Excuse me, excuse me, your honor. I would like to pull that ten thousand dollars surety bail money," and sat back down defiantly and glared at Roger with contempt in my eyes. His face dropped, he was totally shocked. He did not think I would have the resources to get him bail nor did he think I would have the guts to pull it. The judge made an announcement that in light of all the previous charges and this new information he would not be giving bail to this man. He would remain in prison until sentencing. Oh, I felt good that day, revenge was so sweet.

***

A few months passed and I found out I was pregnant. I had been moving on with my life without Roger and things were going quite well until this. I was more than happy to be pregnant again and knew I would have to raise the child on my own. I was okay with that. At least I knew this child would love me as much as I could love him or her. Everyone else had failed me in my life. This was my only way to happiness, I thought. I would give this child all the love and protection it needed. All the things I didn't receive as a child.

Just when I thought I would be alone along came Ross to swoop me off my feet. He had three kids of his own but divorced and the kids were mostly with the wife. Anyway he took me through the birthing process. I was in an extremely hormonal and vulnerable state. Ross was there just at the right time to help out. Once the beautiful baby boy was born I soon realized how incompatible Ross and I were. I also knew I could not give his three kids the love and attention they deserved being a step parent and was not about to do to them what had been done to me by my stepmother, so I asked him to leave.

***

My glorious new baby boy named Tyler was the light of my life. Everything changed that day. After many years of being unfulfilled and along came Tyler. This little boy was so cute and cuddly and all he wanted or needed was his mommy. Finally I could feel loved and significant in my life. I would take Tyler everywhere; just plunk the little guy in a pouch on my chest and off we went. Later the pouch became a stroller and then a seat on the back of my bike.

Although I was enjoying every moment with Tyler I still felt lonely for male companionship. My shoulders weighted with so much guilt about Tyler's father, Roger. "Shouldn't I let him see his son? Will my son be angry that I kept him from seeing him?" All these crazy thoughts were suffocating my mind. And what if I decided to let him see Tyler and he beats him too? Even though I let Roger beat me I could never allow that of my son. The more I focused on these thoughts the more I yearned to see Roger and share our newfound glory together. I focused so hard on all the good thoughts that I could no longer remember all the bad.

I was still friends with some of Roger's friends and they knew I had the baby so I was sure someone would have told him. I put the word out because everyone kept asking me if I had a problem with Roger seeing the baby. In a moment of weakness and vulnerability I gave in. What a momentous day that was. The whole feeling that came with Roger meeting his son for the first time. Being able to see the deep passionate love in his eyes for his son was exalting. This I will never forget as long as I live.

I took photos just in case something happened and I couldn't remember. Also for Tyler's sake so that one day he would see the love in his father's eyes when he saw him for the first time. Everything was so wonderful, all the feelings I had inside about a happy home with mother, father, and baby were exploding out of my chest. Even the thought of my own parents came to light that day, oh, how I yearned for my parents to get back together when I was growing up. I would dream at night and by day of their harmonious reunion and a happy family. Now that this was happening with Roger it just felt right. All the memories of the abuse seemed to go away. I so wanted to believe that things could be different and everything would change.

***

Roger and I decided to make another go of it. Roger promised that he had changed and learned from his mistakes. He explained how he wanted to be a good father to show and give Tyler what he had never had. It all seemed so wonderful to me, it was as if a miracle had happened. Roger moved in with me for a short while. Then we decided to get a place of our own, something with a yard for Tyler to play in when he got older. Tyler was about four months old when he saw Roger for the first time.

Once Roger and I moved into the new place and got settled something started to change. Roger started drinking again with some buddies he met at the Fort. The Fort was a biker's house made into a booze can. Basically a place you could drop in any time, buy a drink real cheap, listen to some tunes and chat with the locals. Anything and everything went on there, drugs, girls you name it. I had gone a few times to meet and party with the guys, following Roger, of course. But most of the time I stayed home with Tyler. Roger's state of mind began to deteriorate with all the drugs and drinking. At first he became verbally abusive, completely loud and obnoxious. I started to fear for my life and Tyler's. What did I do; what was I thinking making the decision to go back with him? Roger would utter evil threats while I pretended to sleep. With a deep angry devious whisper he would say, "I see you lying there, you're not sleeping, I can see your eyes moving. I could kill you, you know."

He was right, I was not sleeping. I would lie there and pretend to be sleeping so as not to aggravate him into abusing me. As my heart pounded loudly in my chest I would try with all my might to keep my eyes shut with little movement. I knew this was not right, I feared for my son's life every waking moment. But Roger wouldn't stop, he would drag me out of bed yelling and screaming at me for pretending to be asleep. He would come up with any excuse he could to beat me once again.

I was feeling worn down; completely depressed about the situation I was in. The more I thought about it the more I believed it was my fate to be abused. It was meant to be. Day after day there were incidences of abuse. Most weeks I sported juicy black eyes which I would have to cover with makeup. There is even a photograph of me and Tyler where the black eye was so bad the makeup couldn't completely hide it.

Finally the day came where everything came to a head; rock bottom, as they say. I was holding Tyler, picking up my bag and getting ready to go out. Roger suspected through his paranoia state that I might be trying to leave him. He was raged. I don't remember much of the words that were said that day no matter how hard I try. All I knew was Tyler's life was seriously in danger. While I was holding Tyler in my arms, Roger began beating me, punching me in the face numerous times. The natural mother's instinct to protect her child was completely expressed in my actions. I leaned Tyler away to the one side away from Roger and pushed my own face towards Roger to take the shots he was giving and save my child from pain.

To this day tears come to my eyes as I remember that day. At that moment, the moment of absolute defeat, it would be my son, at nine months old, that would evidently give me the strength to save my own life. He would give me the leverage that Anthony Robbins spoke about in his tapes that I listened to that would help me make that change. He said, "You must get to a point where, I must change now, I can change now, and I will change now." That point had certainly come for me that day.

I made a decision at that moment that I would leave Roger for good. Prior to that I didn't care, I was okay with the pain being inflicted upon me because deep down I believed I deserved it. Another thing Anthony Robbins spoke about was your belief system.

But, there was no way I would allow anyone to hurt my son. I always had an internal protective system for the underdog anyway. This was so much more than that, this was my baby, the only one in the world who had ever loved me unconditionally. This was my heart connected to his; his pain was my pain. I could feel it so deeply when he cried that it was unbearable. God, Tyler, Anthony Robbins, someone gave me the strength and wisdom to stop and wake up to reality that day. I didn't know who was responsible in the end but all the same I was so grateful.

Now a plan had to be formulated because if Roger knew I planned to leave him he would stop me and beat me again. While the plan was being put into motion I had to pretend that everything was all right. Smiling, laughing, having sex with him when he wanted to, that was the worst part, the whole time trying not to make him mad for any reason. I secretly contacted everyone I thought could help trying to arrange a temporary place to stay and somewhere to store my things. All I could find was a place to store some of my personal items but there was nowhere for me and Tyler to stay until an apartment would be available at my old building. I knew I could no longer keep up this farce and after Roger had beaten me with Tyler in my arms I desperately did not want him to hurt Tyler. We had to leave now.

You are probably wondering why I couldn't stay at my mother's or my sister Jenny who is so kindhearted, surely one of them would be able to help. Well, my mother had been drinking excessively and not paying her bills and was evicted from her apartment. After an attempt of suicide and a stay in the hospital psychiatric ward my mother was placed in a halfway house. She had one bedroom to herself and the rest was shared and always supervised by a staff member so there was no way Tyler and I could go there.

***

Now as for my sister this is a bit complicated. Although my sister loved me dearly she was placed in an extremely awkward position with her husband. You see when I was six months pregnant I was staying at my sister's for a bit. My brother-in-law Byron was a drunk, not physically abusive but to the point he could not speak properly and would try to do things he knew he shouldn't. One of the final incidences occurred at my baby shower. Everyone was giving friendly hugs to the family and friends; nothing unusual. But when I was in the kitchen alone my brother-in-law approached me for his hug and leaned over to give me a kiss. I thought he would kiss me on the cheek which was normal enough but instead at the last second he made contact with my lips and pulled me close and tried to French neck with me by putting his tongue in my mouth. I immediately pulled back and said, "What the hell are you doing?" Of course he was so wasted he could barely express his answer and I walked out of the room.

I was so disgusted, this was my sister's husband. How could he do this? I had felt similar types of sexual innuendos being thrown at me before by him but simply walked away and ignored it hoping it would stop and laying claim on the fact that he was just drunk. But this time was different. I needed to tell my sister. Of course when that happened, the almighty peacemaker, creator of the excuses for his behavior, just fluffed it off. She meant well, Jenny really didn't want her children growing up with the effects of a broken home as she did. Her thoughts and fears of how she would look after her children on her own took over. My sister now pregnant with her second child just a few months further along than me couldn't imagine putting her children through a broken home situation like she had to go through.

So there it stood deep in my mind and now my guard was up and I would watch his every move. Angry that he would take advantage of my sister's kindness and disgusted with his attempts to get closer to me I stored the information in my mind to be retrieved at a later date. It wasn't that much longer when that behavior would arise again and that would be the last straw.

About a month or so later while I was staying at my sister's, partly because I had nowhere to stay and partly to help her out watching her son Charlie when she went into hospital to have her other baby. I remembered it quite vividly, the events that night. My sister had to be taken to the hospital because she was almost ready to deliver. Byron her husband was supposed to go to work but decided he would stay home that night drinking. Again he began to look at me with that same look I remembered before, especially that time in the kitchen. I was not about to stay there and let this situation get out of hand. So I said to Byron, "Since you are staying home and it is my birthday I am going to go out."

Well, that was not what he wanted to hear. He was hoping to prey on me that night knowing full well that my sister would not be there to get in the way. He got angry with me as if I ruined his plans. I had no money and he wasn't about to give me any, so I called my sister in the hospital. Byron automatically, in his paranoid state, thought I was telling my sister his plans. He grabbed the phone from me in an aggressive angry state and began yelling and as I reached for the phone he was swinging it as if to hit me. I snapped. Everything I remembered from my past of men, their abuse, and their demands for sexual favors put me over the edge. When I struggled to get the phone from him he pushed at me and all hell broke loose. The fists went flying and I couldn't stop pounding on him. He tried to fight back but I was winning. There was just too much pent up anger in me that no one was going to take advantage of me again or my sister. As this was all going on Charlie was in the high chair crying and screaming as he saw his father being beaten. My mother who was barely mobile from her obesity managed to fly up from the couch, jumped on Byron's back and got him in a headlock while I continued to beat him.

Finally after several minutes Byron stomped out of the room and went upstairs. I took a moment to calm Charlie down but I was trembling. Six months pregnant and being forced to traumatize my body this way. My mom remained at home and I ran over to Jenny's friend's house to explain what happened and to call my sister. Poor Jenny, here she was in the hospital while her whole family was in disarray. There was nothing she could do. Of course Byron then laid the law down that your sister has to leave and cannot stay here anymore. So this is why Jenny's place was not an option for me and Tyler. Even though my sister and I were speaking whenever we could, there were no visits due to the anger being held by both parties, me and Byron. Unfortunately, Jenny's hands were tied. The only option left for me and Tyler would be to go to a hostel. Anything would be better than risking the life of my son, I thought.

Even though my things could not be picked up with the truck I had arranged until later I knew I had to get out now. With only the items I could carry, Tyler in hand, off I went to the hostel. My heart racing the whole time thinking Roger would come back and kill me. I left a note for him saying we would not be back and why, and that I would later return for my things.

***

When I got to the hostel I realized this was really the bottom of the barrel. Only the extreme desperate people were there. There were six people in a tiny room with only one bed per family, shared bathrooms and minimal food being dispersed. There were people so filthy with lice in their hair and their mental states not intact. Others like me and Tyler who came from abusive relationships and one mother and child whose house had burnt down. The poor child cried every night waking up from nightmares of losing her father in their burning house. You had to leave each day and return at night. They would give you a couple of bus tickets and a bologna sandwich with a piece of fruit to send you on your way. Some of the people were so drugged up that they made you fear for your life and not want to sleep at night. It really was a horrible time for me but I remembered taking strength from this knowing I would not put myself in this position ever again.

When I finally got my apartment Tyler and I began our new life. I hooked up with my old friends in the building and started babysitting to earn some extra money, that way I could be with Tyler.

The worst part about moving out of my place with Roger other than living in a hostel was having to leave most of my things behind to pick up later. Roger called and left a message one day at my dad's, since he had no other number to reach me at to say he was moving out at the end of the month. And if I wanted my things I would need to pick them up before that day. The only day I could arrange to have someone come with a truck was the on the first, which was the same day the new people would be moving in. I called the landlord to explain the situation and pleaded with her to give me until noon to get my stuff out and she agreed.

When I arrived at eleven-thirty in the morning I was devastated to see all of my belongings in open boxes all over the front yard. There were items that couldn't fit in boxes strewn all over. There were people rummaging through my things, thinking it was a garage sale. When I approached one woman standing there held up a phone and asked, "How much do you want for this?" Almost in tears I told the woman that these things were not for sale and sent everyone away.

As the driver waited I held my tears back and searched through the boxes for my most important possessions. Unfortunately there just wasn't enough room in the truck or in the storage unit my friend had agreed to loan me to fit everything, so sadly, I would have to leave some behind. My apartment wouldn't be ready until the end of the month. So I had no choice but to leave some of my things there for people to scavenge through. This was another very difficult day for me.

***

One day when I was babysitting I decided to take the kids out for a walk while the older ones were in school. I put both Mark, my friend's son, and Tyler in the same stroller and off I went. Whenever I went out I would constantly look over my shoulder fearing Roger may try to find me one day. This day was no different than any other. Throughout the walk I spent the whole time on guard while trying to enjoy the walk with the kids.

I was almost home, just about rounding the corner by the bus stop. There were several people standing in and around the shelter waiting for the next bus. Seconds before I was to pass the bus shelter out popped Roger. My heart stopped beating as my breath was taken away and my mouth hung open in shock. He had that look on his face, so terrifying that I remembered all too well. His teeth clenched together as he demanded answers. I quickly moved the stroller into a public place as Roger followed saying, "I will kill you if you run from me."

With stroller in hand I thought quickly and began to deke him out by going left to right and leaving him briefly stuck behind the crowd. I made a run for it to my apartment that was three buildings down. My heart raced frantically, one hand on the stroller as I searched my pocket for my keys not once looking back as I raced to the building. I flew open the first glass door which had no lock and made my way through to the second door. I knew I had only one shot to precisely place the key in the hole as Roger was only seconds behind me.

With desperation and a clear focus and help from the powers that be the key went right in, I pulled open the door and yanked the stroller in then immediately pulling as hard as I could to close the door behind me just seconds before Roger's hand reached the handle. Just as the door shut Roger put his hands on the door. He began banging on the window swearing.

Quickly I hopped on the elevator and ran to my apartment. The kids thought they were getting the ride of their life being raced around in the stroller, while I felt as though I was near death. Upon entering the apartment I immediately picked up the phone and called the police. I was breathing so heavily that I could hardly get the words out. They said they would be right over and to stay put on the phone. It seemed like forever until they arrived but was probably only a few minutes. Roger was long gone by the time they got there.

After an extensive interview with the police, although understanding, they announced there was nothing they could do. Since Roger was not on the scene caught in the act it was my word against his. They suggested for me to go to the justice of the peace to lay charges myself. The police advised me to give their names and let them know it was reported. I had enough of being afraid and this behavior had gone on too long. So I went down to the courthouse, relayed my story and as a result charges were laid of "assault with intent to kill." A peace bond was placed on Roger that he could not go within one hundred yards of me and Tyler or he would be arrested.

Later as a result of that incident, he received a four-year sentence, which ended up being four months because Roger found an error in the judge's ruling and was given an immediate release. Those were the hardest months for me even though I knew what he did was wrong, believe it or not, I actually missed him. That is the sick thing about being in an abused relationship, the one being abused is so emotionally insecure they cannot sustain being alone. They feel they are not worthy of much and begin to rationalize their abuser's behavior while trying to make themselves feel better.

The best thing that happened to me was to be separated

from Roger. Without the ability to call him up or visit him, it gave me time to get to know who I was, begin to care about myself, without the constant manipulation surrounding me, telling me otherwise. When Roger got out of jail he tracked me down again. He said he didn't blame me for reporting him and that he loved me, blah, blah, blah. We saw each other for a few days until Roger started the manipulation again.

As soon as he started blaming me and putting me down it was as if I had been blind and could now see. It was now so clear to me, as he spoke I sat in awe with my eyes and mouth wide open. This enlightenment was so powerful a surge of energy shot through my body and I began to laugh. Laugh, laugh and laugh. I was laughing so hard tears were streaming down my face. Roger became angrier and angrier the more I laughed. He said, "Are you laughing at me? I could kill you for that," spoken through his normal angry gritted teeth. In between laughs, I managed to get my response out, "I am laughing because I can see right through you now. You can no longer manipulate me because I see what you are doing."

From that moment forward our relationship changed forever. Roger and I both went our own ways and only saw each other one more time when Tyler was about three years old. I cannot exactly remember how it started but remembered vividly the middle and the end. We talked and talked most of the night about all the positive old memories. It was as if time stood still and all the bad memories were gone.

We slept naked that one night, holding each other close, with only love and forgiveness in our minds, no sex. Both knew this was our farewell; a chapter had ended in our lives as we gave thanks. The next morning Roger gave Tyler a great big hug goodbye with tears in his eyes. Roger and I hugged as tight as we could, after what felt like years, even decades, passing as we let go of our lives together.

As if in slow motion, our arms brushed together, passing down from our shoulders, to our hands. Our hands met and our eyes locked while thousands of images of our experiences together on this earth passed by. The moment had come, our hands clenched together one final time, not a word was spoken, only a nod to say, thank you. Roger slowly turned and walked away and I closed the door behind him.

That was the last time we saw each other. Even though we were not in touch anymore there were many times in my life where I would draw from my experiences with Roger, both good and bad. It would become the foundation of my strength and then that same strength would be passed on to my son.

CHAPTER TWELVE

DESTINATION LOVE

A lot had changed for Tyler and me that day when I realized I could be loved without pain. The two did not necessarily have to be mixed. Here was this helpless beautiful little boy looking up to me. I was his whole world; there was no pain, only love. I would do anything in my power to protect him and make his life the best it could possibly be. I never cared about myself enough to ever change my situation until Tyler was born. I would change my life for Tyler but not for myself. Although I did not know this at the time but I didn't love myself.

When Tyler was eighteen months I had a revelation. I was home all day babysitting for my friend and one day I suddenly felt like I was in prison. Trapped with moms and tots going through the same routine day in and day out, I needed more. I didn't do anything half assed, I always completely immersed myself in whatever I wanted to accomplish. It was probably due to my extreme lack of patience. I wanted everything now. I did not know what the grey area was, only black or white, high or low. Why that is, I do not know, but it has always been that way for me.

Searching for answers I was looking through the classifieds one day and became extremely disappointed. Every job I looked at required more education or experience that I did not have. Some things I could certainly make up like I had done before with the waitress job, but they were few and far between. Now, my stepmother Mavis and I had become quite close since leaving my father's house many years before. It seemed Mavis no longer felt threatened by me since I did not live there anymore.

Mavis was a very strong black woman from South Alabama. She grew up in the time where blacks were highly mistreated and some were still treated as slaves. They were not allowed to sit at the front of the bus or drink from the same water fountain. She was the eldest of fourteen siblings and as a young girl helped out with farm chores. Mavis always said, "If you're too young to pick cotton, you can always carry water." She participated in many civil rights rallies during her high school years.

After graduation she left her home state of Alabama and went to Buffalo, New York, and then crossed the border to Toronto where she fell in love with the city. Mavis later became a successful Commercial and Residential Realtor.

Even though all odds were against her she managed to become very successful in her life. I liked this and looked up to her. I listened intently when Mavis gave me advice and immediately found a way to apply it. When successful, Mavis would proudly congratulate me for the job, over and over again she would say, "I knew you could do it, I told your father you are a genius and that you are the smartest of his three children." Wow! Nothing made me feel so high, not even drugs could touch that.

There is definitely something about feeling significant, like Anthony Robbins says. There was no question that when I opened the paper that one day and read in despair, that the first person I would call for advice was Mavis. I went through the list of advertisements giving Mavis all the reasons why I could not do them due to my lack of education. I then suggested that maybe I should go back to school. Mavis agreed and asked, "What would you take?"

"What job pays the most money?" I questioned and began reading aloud a list from a school ad in the paper.

Mavis said, "Computers. I think that is high in demand and the pay is good."

So I heeded her advice and went to sign up for school at the Toronto School of Business. They mentioned in the ad that grants and loans were available, so no need to pay upfront. This was great because I did not have any money raising a child on my own. When I arrived at the school for my assessment I was greeted by a polite and friendly woman. As the woman went through the list of questions I sat confidently in my chair while I answered. The first of several questions were about my needs and wants, which I always knew where I stood in this area. Mavis had also helped me to feel that anything was possible at this point. So when the next group of questions came up regarding experience and education I convincingly explained that I learned quickly and begged her to give me a chance to prove myself.

That day was another turning point in my life when I was accepted for training even without meeting the minimum requirements of a grade twelve diploma. The first month of training was a disaster. I had decided to take computer programming, and the material had a lot to do with math, not one of my favorite subjects. Most of the students were fresh out of university and didn't have any trouble with it. I began cutting myself up emotionally telling myself I wasn't smart enough to do this, and what was I thinking. Almost every day as I struggled it ended in tears.

Meanwhile I still had to go home and put a happy face on for Tyler's sake. My stepmother Mavis called near the end of the month and asked how everything was going. I broke down in tears explaining all that had happened. Well Mavis was not one to wallow in self-pity nor was she going to allow me to do so either. As resourceful as Mavis was, she went through all the options she could think of to help solve the problem. Finally she came up with a plan after figuring out that this was possibly not the right course for me. Mavis encouraged me to go and see the school counselor and see if I could switch programs.

After a successful transfer to the microcomputer business applications course I began to excel. Within the last few months of school I was asked to help teach the class and eventually completed the program with honors. Soon after leaving school I got a job as an admin assistant at a credit union. I was well on my way to recovery, making okay money. Tyler was in daycare, which I was able to get a subsidy for because I was a single parent. There were unbelievable resources out there if you looked and fought for them. I had previously received a partial grant and student loan to complete my schooling from the government.

***

After a few months had passed I had long since mastered

the work involved in my job. I had exhausted all of my creative avenues to increase my enthusiasm. I loved my boss, and the people I worked with, but something was missing. My friend Tammy and I decided to take a trip to the Dominican Republic. My mom had been sober for a long time and would babysit when I went out sometimes after work. My mom agreed to watch Tyler for the week while we went away. It would end up being the trip that would change my life forever.

Not only did we have fun and party night after night but I met the man of my dreams. A Dominican man named Jesus. It was love at first sight and quickly progressed from there. Jesus worked at the casino in a nearby resort we frequented. He was the pit boss at the craps table. Tammy and I had no idea how to play craps. While walking past the table I caught the deep brown eyes of Jesus. He quickly smiled and encouraged me to come to play. When I called out my only excuse at playing coy which was, "I don't know how to play." Jesus and his coworkers commented with a well thought out prepared response, "It's okay we can teach you, it's easy, come, we will show you." And that was it... the flirting began and continued as the casino boys let us win. Of course at that time we didn't know they were letting us win until many years later. It didn't matter how anyway, we were glad to count our cash in hand at the end of the night.

As the romance continued, day after day, plans were made for me and Jesus to meet on his day off. At this point, Tammy, not interested in brown men, found herself a couple of tourists to hang out with, giving me and Jesus some time alone. I just couldn't believe it, after so many years of dating off and on only briefly, I finally found true love. He was funny, spoke some broken English, dressed well, good body and absolutely gorgeous. What else could I ask for? I was convinced he was just what I needed.

Before our departure home the two of us exchanged numbers and addresses to keep in contact. When I returned home I was so happy to see Tyler since that was the first time we had ever been apart. My whole world opened up. All I could think about was Jesus, and the Dominican. It was wonderful to be treated like a queen, to have a man drooling at my feet, looking up at me with starry eyes. I loved Tyler with all my heart, but somehow I needed adult male companionship in my life as well. Even though for years, in order to survive, I told myself otherwise.

Since I was already unhappy, or bored you could say, in my job, my mind was racing for some fulfillment, excitement, balance, I didn't know. Every waking moment I thought about this strange man I met on vacation. We wrote letters and sent them by fax. I ran my phone bill up talking to him. Long distance relationships can be very costly. Jesus explained to me the rules of his government and that they would not let the people out, even to visit, when I asked him to come to Canada. Only the ones who have lots of money and were established businessmen were allowed to go. This was because the government was fairly confident those people would come back.

You see, the Dominican Republic being a Third World country, mostly run by the cheap labor of their many citizens, consists of the poor and the rich, no middle class. It was all very confusing for me, since I had not seen the news or read a newspaper in many years. Not that I did not have access to it, I just simply refused, I felt there was enough despair and sadness in my own life to deal with. So there really was no need to add more shit to the pile, as they say. Besides, it would make me feel very sad for the people who were in pain from their losses. I just couldn't take it.

With this in mind you can imagine my naivety to the outside world and what really went on. My family tried to warn me about my involvement with Jesus. Stubborn as I was I would not allow any of it to enter my mind. He made me feel good and that was all that mattered. After a couple more visits to the Dominican Republic, and numerous phone calls and fax communications, I couldn't take it anymore. I yearned for his partnership, and could not wait any longer, so I decided I would move to the Dominican Republic.

Jesus warned me that I would not like it there. That it was much different than Canada and it did not have the amenities I was used to. He said, "There is no running water here, the government shuts off the power for most of the day, it's very hot etc. etc. etc." I thought briefly about all of that, and figured that it was time for me to have a simpler life. How difficult could it be to not have running water, and I loved the heat and hated the winters, so it was perfect. I wasn't too happy about the government taking large chunks of change from my pay checks for taxes either. I loved the Spanish language, and the Dominicans were so friendly, unlike the Canadians. By the time I was done I had convinced myself that Tyler and I would be better off moving there.

So the announcement was made, I told my family I was getting married and moving to the Dominican Republic in six weeks. I quit my job, sold most of my possessions, leaving some personal things with my family to pick up later. I couldn't be more excited with the decision I had made.

May 1989: Tyler and I along with my mother arrived in the Dominican Republic for a wedding and a move. We had the hotel booked for the first two weeks, which gave me and Jesus time to look for a place to rent. The wedding was beautiful. Tyler was there as ring bearer, all dressed up in a Spanish suit. My mom was in tears the whole time, as parents often do when their kids get married and are leaving home. The wedding was very simple, yet extravagant for the Dominicans. A limo came to pick the bride up to take me to the wedding. I was so blindly in love I did not even notice it was a beat up old Cadillac with a dent in the side until the photos came back a few weeks later.

Any type of car in the Dominican was a luxury, even more so if it was a large vehicle. The man who was driving it was some kind of captain in the Army, so he was all decked out in a white uniform with the hat. The energy filled the air and charged through my body. Tyler was misbehaving as usual, not really adjusting to this new country I had taken him to. The church ended up being some kind of community hall. When the car pulled up alongside a wire fence the only way you could tell it was a wedding was all of the people dressed up standing outside. There were some Spanish words above the entrance which of course I did not understand and it really didn't matter I was so smitten with Jesus I did not even care.

The ceremony was completely in Spanish. After several minutes of gibberish from the justice of the peace I was given a quick nudge from Jesus' sister as if to say it is your turn to speak now. I was completely dumbfounded and I could not remember what they had told me I was to say. When everyone realized this, Jesus' sister then whispered to me, "Yo accepto." I smiled as I suddenly remembered my lines and repeated the words, "Yo accepto." Technically I did not know what I was accepto-ing to, but went ahead with it anyway. For those of you who do not understand Spanish "yo accepto" means I do, or I accept. Pretty scary to accept something and sign papers in Spanish totally putting your trust in a bunch of strangers when you understand very little Spanish. People will do some crazy things in order to fulfill their need for love. When they say that love is blind they really do mean that you walk forward even though you cannot see.

When the ceremony was over, Jesus and I exited the building arm in arm as bride and grooms do, while people threw rice at us. This was pretty much the only part of all of this that Tyler liked, understandably so since all the children were trying to talk to him but he did not know a word of Spanish, and was frustrated. And now his mother was hand-in-hand with someone other than him. Not so good. Major jealousy happening. Needless to say, there are a few photos in action as I tried to control him and he angrily defied me.

Everyone went to Jesus' aunt's house for the reception. It looked beautiful. Amazing what can be done with a few pink and white sheets, some ribbons and few other things from around the house. When you're in love I don't think the bride and groom need much, it's the attendees who want all the hoopla. All I cared about was being in love, finding a good man to be a father to my son, and to share my life with. After some drinks and the traditional activities such as the cutting of the cake, drinking wine with our arms locked together, and throwing the bouquet, it was now time for the bride and groom to go on their honeymoon.

So you see these traditions are pretty much the same

around the world. Tyler and his grandmother were brought back to the resort, while the bride and groom, Jesus and I, went to a nearby hotel. I guess when you are in paradise, no need to go anywhere else. The honeymoon was short and sweet, just the one night in the hotel, and then back to searching for a place to live as time was running out. Finally, we found a room we could rent with a shared bathroom and kitchen.

After the second week passed I said my goodbyes to my mother as she left to return home without her daughter and grandson. There were so many tears we could have filled a river. Even though my mother and I fought constantly, we really loved each other. For the past ten years we had always lived close to one another; no more than a few blocks. Now we would be oceans apart. After that goodbye and returning to the rented room, it all started to sink in, "Oh my God, this was real," I thought, "Now what?"

Jesus and I talked about finding me a job. He explained what the pay was like at the average job, assuming I spoke Spanish. Since I did not speak it very well this would propose some major difficulties to overcome. Prior to leaving Canada I had made several attempts to be hired from Canada. Jesus had mentioned that if I was brought in to work from outside the Dominican the companies would pay me in US dollars, which would work out to be a lot more. I submitted my resume at places like IBM; however, I faced the same dilemma of not being able to speak the country's official language. Jesus found a job where I could work at the casino as an assistant to the high rollers. Basically, I would have to get them whatever they wanted. Not only was the pay really low, I would also need to speak the language enough to make the calls and set things up. Besides all of that, who would look after Tyler. There really was no one offering and I was very protective of Tyler in this foreign country and didn't want anything to happen to him. It was now time for Jesus to go back to work.

Here we were left sitting in a room with barely any electricity because the government would shut the power off most of the day. There were several single, grungy men, who rented rooms in the same house. Jesus gave strict instructions not to trust them and to stay as far away from them as possible. This made things extremely difficult for me and Tyler, sitting in a room with two single beds, a small end table and no TV. There was a shared bathroom down the hall with a toilet and no toilet seat. A tub and shower with a glass sliding door but no running water. Just a bucket of cold water sitting inside with a cup to use to pour the cold water over your head and body to get clean. Down the hall, a shared kitchen but with no electricity half the time, and there was nothing in the fridge. I was too scared to go outside without Jesus because I did not speak the language good enough, plus the fact that I looked like a foreigner and the impoverished Dominicans would prey on me for whatever they could get. It was extremely hot, temperatures in the high nineties and without electricity there was no fan or air conditioning. Whenever Jesus was home I would have him go with me to the bathroom to protect me from the men because there was no lock on the bathroom door. Worst of all, there were cockroaches, bigger then you could possibly imagine, about the size of your foot and they fly.

One night there was one on the nightstand in the room. You could hear it shuffling along. We banged on the table hoping the noise would scare it off. No way, it did not give a shit. To kill it would make a disgusting crunching noise while all the guts spurted out. Jesus got rid of that one as

Tyler and I hid on the other side of the room. As for sleeping, at night it was almost impossible. It was so hot it was completely unbearable. The fear of more cockroaches coming in and maybe crawling all over us was an added pressure. In the meantime any time we had available we looked for a better place to stay. I was terrified to go to the bathroom without Jesus being present. He would scout out for any bugs and then guard the door while me and Tyler went to the bathroom or shower.

Finally Jesus found a relative who would rent us a room in their house, a little safer to leave us alone while he worked. But still no electricity, so the nights were very hot. There were no screens on most houses there because people would steal them and they were very expensive to buy. Same as the toilet seats, so without screens the mosquitoes would eat you alive at night. Tyler and I were completely covered in bites the size of quarters. Tyler would cry daily from the itch and heat. He hated the Dominican. When he was thirsty I would tell him how to ask for water from the relatives. Tyler would stomp his feet and say, "I don't want to speak Spanish."

Each day got worse and worse and I became quite ill. Even though we mostly drank pop and did not eat salads because they may have been washed with the contaminated water, I still got sick. I had diarrhea so bad that at night I couldn't make it to the toilet. It gushed out of me like water all the way down the hall. The only way to flush the toilet was to dump a bucket of water in it. After so many visits to the toilet I had used up all the well water. Feeling completely embarrassed, knowing his relatives would get up and see all the mess, I just wanted to crawl under a rock. I pleaded with Jesus to refill the water, but it was so dark out and Jesus did not know where the well was, so he couldn't do it.

Weeks passed and I was still sick. I had burned my leg on the side of the motorcycle taxi we took to travel to the next town. At night when we walked outside we had to stomp our feet on the ground to stop the rats from crawling up our legs. There were no streetlights, and the roadsides were covered in garbage, so the rats were having a fiesta.

Finally after six weeks, still no job, my money nearly out, I was considering going back home to Canada. The three of us went to the Canadian Consulate to apply for Jesus to come to Canada. Jesus said it should be easier now that we were married. While walking down the sidewalk Jesus grabbed me at the last second and pulled me back, right below only one step ahead was a manhole with no lid. No signs to indicate that only seconds later I would drop twenty feet down. All the little things I noticed were very different to Canada. Ultimately realizing that I took a lot of things for granted. The application was submitted and I had booked my flight back with Tyler. We would wait for Jesus to come to Canada when the government approved his papers. But for now I could not bear another day in this horrible impoverished country.

After arriving back on Canadian soil, I dropped to the ground and kissed it. I thanked the taxman under my breath for providing the extra services I had taken for granted. For the little things like being able to run water from the tap that you can drink. Having a hot shower instead of buckets of cold water, sleeping with a fan at night when it's hot without having to worry about mosquitoes because now you have screens. Garbage picked up and put in the dump, no rats crawling about or cockroaches that fly. Not having to worry that someone will steal your purse off your shoulder as you walk on a busy street. The availability of an ambulance if needed, where the option in the

Dominican Republic is to dump the body on a wooden flatbed hooked up to a vehicle to transport you to wherever. There were many lessons learned by me and I knew I was ready to stay in Canada but now I had a much better appreciation for my country, the government and my family.

CHAPTER THIRTEEN

FIGHTING FOR MY SON

Things were not that simple after my return to Canada. Since we had no apartment left to move back to, ultimately, we had nowhere to stay. We temporarily moved in with my mother. However, my mother was only in a bachelor apartment, which meant just a combined living room, bedroom, kitchen and a small separate bathroom. First of all, there was not enough room for two adults and one child, and the landlord had rules of only one person in a bachelor. Well, it was only for a short while, I thought, hoping I could get welfare or unemployment to help me financially to get back on my feet.

Unfortunately, it had been several months since I quit my job to move to the Dominican Republic, and normally I would have to apply for unemployment insurance right away. Also, they would not be too fond of the fact that I left the country. I quickly came up with a plan: I would ask my old boss who knew I was leaving the country, not to mention that part if unemployment insurance called to verify. My ex-boss was very hesitant and said she could not lie for me. I pleaded with her while tears poured down my face, telling her that my situation with my mom was grim, and that my son and I would soon have no income, and nowhere to live. Donna, my old boss said, "I am sorry. I wish I could help you, but I just can't lie to the government."

I hung up the phone and continued crying for hours. I was devastated and was prepared to give up. I knew I did not have any more options left. My mother was screaming at me daily saying, "You need to get out of here or I will be kicked out." After regaining my composure, I continued to look for work. I had applied for unemployment insurance, but was denied for quitting my old job and leaving the country. Welfare told me to go to unemployment insurance because I should be eligible since I was working before, and they refused to give me any more money. What was I to do?

At the bottom of the barrel, I prayed to God to please save Tyler and me from this despair. I always really believed that God would help me. That faith certainly carried me through some desperate times. Several days later, a letter appeared under my mother's door from the landlord. It said something to this effect: "The rental contract you signed, and that the approval was based on, states there will be only one person living in this apartment. Some new information has been brought to our attention, indicating there is more than one person living in your apartment. Take this letter as a warning, that we will evict you if the additional people are not removed from the premises immediately."

What would I do now? Where would we go without money or a job, my mother getting angrier by the second and much more verbally abusive? Just as all of these thoughts were running rampant through my mind, the phone rang. It was Donna, my old boss. She said, "I have a proposition for you.

Since you know I have already hired someone for your position when you left, I cannot give you back your old job. But I was thinking, I would like to hire you to train her because she is not doing as good a job as you were. Maybe you could teach her how to use the computer better. It wouldn't be permanent, but it could help put some money in your pocket."

I was so grateful I could not stop telling Donna how much I appreciated her kind, thoughtful, gesture. I immediately made arrangements with my mother to babysit Tyler and off to work I went. After a couple of weeks training Donna's new assistant, other staff members passed by wanting to know what I was doing. When they heard that I was providing training, they wanted some too. Computers were very new to all of the staff and no one really had any formal training. Donna raved about my success with Shannon, her assistant, to upper management and suggested they create a more permanent position for me.

With Donna's influence, and the power of the requests coming in from all of the staff, a position was created. I was offered and accepted the position of "Personal Computer Specialist." The job offered a much higher pay than I was getting before I quit, plus I would have full benefits. This gave me the ability to get my own apartment just up the road from my mother. It was a cute, upper floor of an old house, on Maynard Avenue. There were two bedrooms, a large living room, a separate kitchen and bathroom. This is where we would stay while we waited for Jesus to arrive in Canada. It was still very difficult, waiting and yearning for him to come, but I no longer had the burning desire to leave my country. I applied for daycare subsidy, but there was a long waiting list, so my mother watched Tyler while I went to work for now.

My new job kept me very busy. I felt so important there, with everyone complimenting me on my good work. Not only did I conduct one-on-one training, but I also started running my own classes and creating training material for the students. Up to this point in my life, this was the best job I had ever had. I loved every aspect of it. It was constantly challenging, with new projects being created, while an implementation of a computer network was established. I travelled to all thirteen branch locations to conduct training. After numerous phone calls to a variety of government organizations, immigration finally gave the green light for Jesus to come to Canada.

***

This was an incredible time for me. It had seemed like an eternity of waiting. And now the time had finally come, one year later, around June 24, 1991. I videotaped the first week of his arrival, right from the airport when he landed his feet on Canadian soil. Tammy, who was my best friend at the time, did the recording, while Tyler and I nervously hid behind a pole to surprise Jesus. When he got off the plane and grabbed his luggage Tammy soon had him in view of the camera. He looked so nervous, but tried to look confident as he walked out the gate. Jesus frantically scanned the crowd to find me. When at first he could not see me, I am sure he was starting to panic thinking, "What if she doesn't show up, what will I do?"

As the camera followed him around, he looked at it several times wondering why this person was taping him. Out from our hiding spot, Tyler and I came running over to embrace Jesus. Tammy was sure I would cry when I saw him, and even bet me five bucks I would. I held back as much as I could not to lose the bet, but inside, I really wanted to let it all out. After patiently waiting over a year for his arrival, of course this day would be emotional. All my hopes and dreams of finally having a decent father figure for Tyler would come to fruition. I could also have someone to love me, without abuse. The first week was so exciting for me as I showed Jesus, a man who only knew life in a Third World country, how wonderful it was to be in Canada. He seemed truly as excited as I was. He danced and sang, as we visited all the famous sights of Toronto.

First, we went for a boat ride on my dad's police boat. Again, Jesus seemed genuinely grateful for his new life. Tyler was thrilled to have a dad to hang out with. We visited Center Island and Jesus and Tyler experienced the log ride, tearing down the waterfalls in a cutout tree log, screaming. I don't think Jesus had any idea the extent of beauty and excitement Canada had to offer. Even I gained a deeper appreciation for the attractions I took for granted after watching the expression on Jesus' face. With my sister and nephews and niece we saw the CN Tower, the largest structure in the world. Up over 200 floors in a glass elevator we moved to the top of the tower. Jesus could not believe his eyes.

Everything was so perfect, until six weeks later when it all came crashing down. I knew that Jesus would not be able to find a job because he did not speak English well enough, and he did not have a trade, or a transferable skill acceptable to Canadian standards. Since I had lost my daycare subsidy when I moved to the Dominican, there was a waiting list to get Tyler back into daycare. I had a brilliant idea; I figured Jesus could babysit Tyler in the daytime, while I worked, then Jesus could go to school at night to learn English. He did not seem very happy about that. He responded almost with disgust, as if I was asking him to do something horrible. I loved Tyler so deeply; I would not allow anyone to hurt him. Jesus explained, "Men don't take care of the kids in my country." I was offended, and felt as though he did not care enough for my son to treat him right.

My suspicions were growing stronger regarding who Jesus really was. Only the week before, I had been looking at his papers from immigration for details to fill out on the school application, when I found something that just didn't sit right with me. There, listed on his paperwork, were his two children's names, which I knew about from the beginning. What I did not know about was their birth dates. When I compared the two children's birthdates, I realized, they were less than nine months apart. How could that be? This meant these children must have been born from two different women. Jesus had never said that. He had always led me to believe that these children came from the same mother. When I questioned him, he pretended not to understand English enough to respond. Nothing was worse for me than not being able to communicate. Being the outspoken person I was, I always knew that communication was the key to any relationship. Jesus began ignoring me, staring at the TV. I was furious with this and turned the TV off and grabbed the remote from him.

So you can see, how a week later, hearing Jesus' reaction to watching my child, went deep to the heart. I thought this man lied to me about his children, and he wanted to send money back home to the family, which I didn't have. To top it off, he got upset when I asked him to take care of my son. Suddenly a light went on in my head. I realized that I really didn't know this man. I scanned through my brain of all the prior incidents where lies or false perception may have been. Once there is suspicion, your mind then conjures up all kinds of things. By the time my mind had finished creating stories, I could no longer be with this strange man.

Out of fear of the unknown, I began sleeping in Tyler's room, with a baseball bat. I had informed Jesus that he should go back to his country and he was not welcome here. I even went to a lawyer for a divorce one day. And by the time I got home, Jesus had packed his things and moved out of our apartment. In some senses, I was relieved; however all I really wanted was the truth. I wanted Jesus to communicate with me and let me know what was going on in his head. The end result would probably still have been the same, but I would not have been left with so many unanswered questions, forcing me to carry more anger about men for many years to come.

The main reason for my decision to break up with him came down to my son. I had promised myself after Roger beat me with Tyler in my arms, that no one would ever come close to hurting my loving son again.

I kept adding bricks, each time something like this happened, to barricade men from getting into my vulnerable heart. I focused on my career and raising Tyler. Yes, I dated off and on after that, but not seriously, and mostly on my own time. I knew I would have to make a commitment to spare my child from any more pain. It was too late, because Tyler had already been affected by the incident with Roger, and I did not realize it until sometime later.

Tyler would act out in many circumstances, loaded with energy since daycare. He bit a child's cheek so hard it made a mark and bruises. I didn't think much about it at first. I thought this was a result of teaching him to protect himself.

You see when he was young; I decided to teach my son not to let anyone take advantage of him. I remembered the many years of suffering I endured, when I was in school and people would tease me. No one was a tattletale in those days, they just fought back, to show their opponent they could stand up for themselves, and that they would not let anyone push them around. This is something that had been passed down through generations. My parents used to say, "If you let people push you around, then they will always do it. If you stand up for yourself, win or lose, you gain respect."

Now that would not work in today's society, since children are now brandishing knives and guns, but for the most part, in my era of growing up this system worked, and it helped me survive. So naturally, I would pass this on to my son, not understanding there were other things going on in Tyler's mind.

Once Tyler went to school, the situation got even worse. First, in junior kindergarten, Tyler had tripped on the edge of the carpet at home, and hit his face just under his eye, on the corner of a floor model speaker. It was quite bruised, and when he went to school the teacher asked, "What happened?" Tyler initially told her that his mother beat him up. Well, lights went on for the young teacher, thinking, this poor child is living in an abusive home, and she called the Children's Aid to report it. So, of course they were obligated to investigate the incident.

The Children's Aid Society interviewed Tyler at school, and then came to my house to ask questions and look around. Now, I was tough, being a single mother, but I was by no means an abusive parent. I gave everything from my heart and soul to Tyler. When the Children's Aid Society came to inspect, and after a series of questions, they realized this was the case. Also, by the time all this had happened, Tyler had relayed several other stories to explain the same incident. He had said a bad man came and pushed him down on the curb outside the school, and then the boogie man hit him with a pipe and so on.

With this information, and the fact that our home was clean and organized, and I was working and spoke intelligently, they realized the claim had no merit. Weeks later, the same teacher asked him to put away his chair. He refused, and picked up the chair and threw it at her. This was reported to me as a serious concern about Tyler's behavior. That is when I realized, something wasn't right.

I spent countless hours researching childhood behaviors and methods to work with him. Nothing seemed to be working. I arranged for an assessment to be done with the school board psychiatrist. They did a series of testing on Tyler like hearing, and one that stands out vividly in my mind. He had given Tyler some building blocks with letters on it and asked him to build something with it. Tyler took the blocks and instead of building the highest tower possible like most other children the psychiatrist had tested, he spelled out words. The psychiatrist was astonished and told me, "No child has ever done this at his age," which was four at the time, in all the years of his practice. I was proud of Tyler for this and felt he was more intelligent than the teachers could see. So psychologically, according to the doctor, he was not developmentally delayed.

The area of behavior would then need to be assessed by someone else, a psychologist. However, there was a long waiting list for this, but I added his name to it anyway. I wanted answers, and to provide the best help for Tyler while he was young. While Tyler would be jumping around constantly, making noises, and rarely sitting still, many people said he was probably hyperactive, so I continued to do more research into this area. In grade one; one and a half years later, just before Tyler's appointment to be assessed, Tyler tried to stab the teacher with some scissors. Again this was brought to my attention. The teacher was not very elegant in how she presented her thoughts. She told me that, "Tyler is crazy and he has mental issues."

Well, this completely fired me up, and my blood began to boil. I laid right into her saying, "Are you a psychiatrist?"

And when the teacher responded, "No," I said, "You are not qualified to say those things about my son." I went to the principal to complain and to demand Tyler be put with a different teacher. I gave an ultimatum that Tyler would not be returning to school, until this teacher was removed. I also wrote a letter to the superintendent of the Board of Education to express my thoughts. A week later, I was called by the principal to say that the teacher was no longer there and that Tyler could return to school.

This was also the time, when Tyler was seven years old, that he was provided with a big brother from the Big Brothers organization. I had applied about a year earlier thinking this might help him to have a male figure in his life. Tyler's "Big Brother" was a police officer named Scott Mills. As a big brother Scott was required to commit to a minimum of one year of making one visit per week to help provide support, friendship, and guidance to a boy without a father. Scott was perfect; they couldn't have chosen a better match for Tyler. Although I do not mention a lot about all the trials and tribulations of Tyler's life in this story, I feel it is important to point out the significance of Scott in our lives. Scott not only provided moral support for Tyler, he also helped me to cope with the many issues I had regarding Tyler. We could call Scott any time of day or night and he would be there for us.

Even though he was only required to volunteer his time as a big brother for one year, Scott has remained in Tyler's life to this day and continues to be an important part of our family. Throughout Tyler's teenage years when he had dealings with the law, Scott was there to provide love and direction. He played an integral part in Tyler's perception of the police department and the legal system. Scott also helped Tyler differentiate between right and wrong in a time of great need. In addition, he helped Tyler to understand and appreciate the magnitude of the love I had for him. I am sure this story would have taken a completely different route had Scott not been in our lives. Again here is another person who moved through our lives for a purpose.

I am telling you all of this so you know that, even though I was completely messed up with my love relationships with men, there was no question of my love for my son and what I would do to protect my child. Why couldn't I put it together and find that same love among men. It would be many years before any light would be shown upon this area.

Tyler was finally assessed and I was given the report that my son had ADHD (attention deficit hyperactivity disorder). The natural suggestion of the doctor was to put Tyler on some medication, a pill called Ritalin. I was not fond of medication as a solution to anything, since I had watched my mother with a shopping bag full of pills the doctor had given her. One to counteract the other, and my mother was always sick and overdosing on them. I was extremely hesitant with this option for my child. The specialist made a strong case and promised me it would only be temporary. So reluctantly I agreed, knowing at the time that I was at my wit's end with Tyler's behavior at home and the teachers were feeling the same at school.

I bought books on ADHD to learn all about it. I immersed myself in whatever information was out there. I applied all the behavior techniques, making lists, applying reward systems, etc. But nothing seemed to work. The doctors of course lied and Tyler was still on the pills several months later. Only now he was like brain dead; he became depressed looking like he was tired all the time. I kept asking the doctor questions, reporting all these side effects. Then he would modify the dosage saying, "This was a normal transition period." Tyler attended counseling sessions in addition that I had also arranged.

I felt that there must be something else that could be done, instead of pills. In my heart, I truly believed this very strongly. Another enlightening moment occurred while Tyler was in counseling. He had mentioned to the counselor that he would have nightmares, which I knew about, but didn't think too much of it. My biggest concerns were the aggressive outbursts, violence, and the pictures he drew of people killing other people. He never drew a house, clouds or the sun, always angry pictures. The counselor brought me in to question me, and to give me an assessment. She asked, "How long has your son been having nightmares?"

I replied, "For many years. I can't recall when it actually started." The counselor then asked me if I was in an abusive relationship. I responded, "Not now, but when Tyler was an infant."

She asked if Tyler asked about his father, and I quickly replied, "No, I don't think he remembers, as he was only eighteen months old." Now, here is the enlightening moment, the counselor said that children, even though they cannot communicate these incidents, do remember them and feel them. These memories will come out in the form of nightmares. In the daytime when they are awake, they will often ask questions in a roundabout way about the perpetrator in their dreams. For example, Tyler might say, "Is that person my daddy?" pointing to a complete stranger to see how I react. If I was standoffish or abrupt with my actions or words, the child, Tyler in this case, would then retaliate internally, knowing this topic is something that upsets me. "Wow, that totally made sense," I thought.

The counselor instructed me to watch and be aware of these sideways questions, and to talk to Tyler about his dad, and tell him all about him. Then he will realize it is not just his imagination, and that he is safe now. This will enable him to find some closure. This totally made sense to me, and in hopes of helping to cure my son I would try anything. The counselor also suggested a special program for Tyler at school. I had been fighting for this, but without some professionals to back my claim, they would not give the approval since funding was limited.

I had a long road ahead of me as a single parent with a child who needed extra help. But all my love and attention went towards Tyler. I had built up a brick wall around me for protection and no man was getting in. I honestly felt I did not need a man in my life. My only positive experiences with love had been with my son. I could love him unconditionally, and he would love me back. No matter what hardship we went through, we would always love each other. This was what I wanted in a relationship with the men I had been with. This was what I was searching for, and now it was too late. The longer I remained single, the more my focus went on Tyler, someone who would love me back, and the more I closed off that other side of me. As for the sex part of a relationship, it really didn't matter. There was always some "stiff cock, has no conscience" type of guy who would jump at the opportunity, if I wanted it. This was not as important for me. I had experienced just about everything in that area in the past, as a result, only giving me grief in the end. The only positive thing that ever came out of that situation was the birth of my son.

Throughout the years, while Tyler was growing up, there were many, many happy fun times we shared. He brought me such joy and satisfaction in my life. I always believed he would do well in his life, despite the difficulties he faced with his ADHD, school, and his friends. I applied the same belief system that carried me through my own life to his. Whenever Tyler would say, "I can't do it," I would say, "Yes you can," hoping to instill a strength and confidence in him to succeed, no matter what the consequences.

I knew anything was possible. Look at me. Here I was, a person who grew up with such a troubled childhood, watching the abuse with my mother, being molested at four years old, living in the Children's Aid Society, surviving a corrupted use of drugs and violence, to living on the streets, and finally being locked up in a reform school with the worst of the worst. Let us not forget, the many abusive relationships with men I endured, when I thought my life would be over at any time.

Now I was a respected parent, in the authorities' eyes, especially the school and psychologists. Most other parents were so messed up and that was half the reason their kids were the way they were. I was a personal computer specialist, with a large credit union, making pretty good money, especially for a woman at that time. I not only participated in all aspects of Tyler's road to improvement, but I most often was the initiator. Desperate to help him succeed, I found whatever programs were available, monitored and altered his diet. I put him in activities like karate, baseball, and soccer to help him release his excess energy and find something he was good at, so that he could gain confidence.

For some reason, I knew, if I believed I could do something, then I could. No matter what knowledge or experience I had previously. I had proved this many times in my own life. Remembering back to when I got the job as a waitress at Bobbi Jo's. I believed wholeheartedly that I could do it, even though I had never done it before. First of all, I was under the legal drinking age and not legally able to drink liquor, never mind serve it. But that didn't stop me. I borrowed one of my friend's identification and went to apply as Crystal. Within three weeks the manager came to me and said, "Crystal, "I know that a lot of people lied on their applications, but you were not one of them." He said he could tell by the great work I did that I was experienced and even offered me the job of head waitress. I carried this experience with me throughout my life, and would draw upon it any time I thought I couldn't do something.

Later through my studies of Anthony Robbins and personal power I realized this was the basis of his teachings. He would ask, "What are the two reasons people do things?" And then say, "They either do it because it will give them pleasure, or they avoid it because of fear of failure." That is because your belief system tells you this. If you change your belief system like I did with the waitress job, "you can do it." I believed wholeheartedly, I was a waitress before I ever did it, so well, that I excelled. It's pretty amazing when you think about it.

So you see with Tyler, no matter what excuse he came up with why he could not do something, I would shut it down and say, "You can do it, yes you can." I would drill this into his head over and over again. I bet you if you asked Tyler today, what did your mother used to say to you when you said you can't do something, he would blurt out that saying.

Although for many years to follow, I used my relationship with Tyler as the basis of my strength, knowing he could not be by my side forever. One day he would grow up and need to go on his own journey in life, which is exactly what happened. I won't go into too many details of how he got there as this would be another book in itself but what you should know is that it was an extremely difficult road where Tyler and I accomplished great feats to get there.

CHAPTER FOURTEEN

HEALING

Here are the events that led to that day. Tyler was out of control, on drugs, and eighteen years old. He was verbally abusive to me when he did not get his own way. Tyler would be out most of the time with his friends, and I would be alone at home. Somehow that security blanket I had with Tyler was dissipating and I needed more. I was working for the past four years for the government in Ontario, teaching a proprietary program, making about four hundred dollars a day. The project had come to an end, as all the employees around the province had been trained. I became severely depressed, I would try looking for work, but I was unsuccessful. For days I would not leave the house, or even get dressed. I felt my life was slipping away. The more Tyler got upset with me, the worse I felt. Tyler was getting into more and more mischief with his friends, and I had no control. I also thought about the jobs that were available; they were so far to get to. It seemed my life would be spent mostly traveling to and from work, and no one would pay me what I was used to. "How much further down could I go?"

Just when I thought I was at the bottom of the barrel where my emotions and health were concerned, I realized I wanted a more peaceful life. The hustle and bustle of Toronto, the long hours driving in traffic, was not making me feel good anymore. I loved my sister Jenny dearly and we had become very close over the years, inseparable actually, and best friends in the truest sense. However, Jenny was in a not-so-good relationship with her husband, who was an alcoholic. Her children did not show her any respect, and I could not take standing by watching my sister being hurt like that. I needed to get away from it all, or I was afraid I would say or do something I would regret later. Now, whether this was the whole reason, or just my mind's way of making me believe it was a solution, I don't know. What I did know was that I was pretty in tune with my senses. You know when people talk about gut instinct, that is what I'm talking about. I even studied spiritual development for three years at my church. It was a different kind of church, this one was the spiritual church, where people from all religious followings could attend. The one common belief was that there was life after death. What that meant was, when you die, or your body dies, your soul or spirit lives on, and can communicate with you through messages. Sometimes relayed through a medium, and if you are listening close enough, through you.

I got so good at it I would stand on the podium at the church and as spirit told me messages, I would give them to others. I only wished that I had been more in tune in my teen years, as I may not have put myself in certain situations, if I had been listening to my gut.

I knew I had this ability as a child when the foster father at the Children's Aid Society was molesting me. I just knew it wasn't right. At the church, they believed everyone has this capability, but they just filled their minds with so much other information growing up, that they forget they have it, or they just aren't listening. Sometimes the messages were so strong I couldn't help but hear them.

One message in particular came to mind. I woke up one morning and suddenly felt a relief in my being. I had decided I would move to British Columbia. You see my father had retired there with my stepmother years before. I had visited a few times, and felt it was so calming to be there. I really had no idea at the time why I needed to go there, but I knew I did.

I told my sister that Tyler and I would be moving to British Columbia in six weeks. My sister thought I had lost my mind, coming up with such a dramatic plan. Although I did not really know why when Jenny asked me, I soon came up with all kinds of reasons to explain. You see, this was the only way most normal people would accept such out of the ordinary things, if they had a logical explanation as to why. We had a massive garage sale three weeks in a row, selling most everything we owned, keeping only a few personal items like clothes and pictures, which we shipped to my dad's temporarily.

This was my last hope for sanity, and to save my son from the corruptive direction he was heading in. Off I went six weeks later, with my son at six-foot-one, our Labrador retriever dog named, "Hailey," and a few personal items all packed into a Honda Civic hatchback. There was barely enough room to breathe, let alone anything else. Five days and nights of traveling across Canada, while I would drive for about eight hours a day, and then rest at a hotel for the nights.

It was exciting at first, but Tyler kept falling asleep along the way. So he wasn't much company for me. Hailey hated the car; she would whine and cry most of the time, I had to give her Gravol™ to calm her down. When I hit the flat lands of the prairies through Saskatchewan, I began getting tired while driving. Not a good thing, since Tyler and the dog were sleeping. For fear of falling asleep at the wheel, I decided to pull over. There was a lining of bush leading to some kind of park I saw and thought that it would be the perfect place to have a nap. Now this Honda Civic I had did not have any air-conditioning, so I cracked open the window for some air and fell asleep. Later I awoke to the sounds of Hailey crying in my ear, and mosquito bites all over us. It was the year of the worst mosquito population in Saskatchewan, nothing better than a car full of fresh blood sitting by their homes in the bush, they must have thought. I quickly got all the mosquitoes out of the car, and started heading back on the road.

Tyler was cramped and cranky, and so was the dog, most of the way. If they weren't sleeping, they were bitching. Needless to say, the road trip part was not as exciting as I originally thought it would be, but even so, I had no doubts that this was my destiny. I was excited because I knew inside there was something greater for me out there.

***

After a long grueling trip, we finally arrived in British Columbia just outside my dad's place. The three amigos pealed themselves out of the hot car, relieved to have finally arrived. I do not remember much about how we got along for the two weeks prior to finding our own place, all I knew was the dog's urine wrecked my dad's lawn. He was very good about it at the time, but for years later I would hear about how the dog wrecked patches of the lawn and he had to cut them out and replace it.

Well I did find my dream home, a beautiful, A-frame house, at the edge of the forest. It had a loft, with massive windows to look out onto the natural landscape, and a huge front veranda, which spanned the full length of the house. Hailey was in heaven with mounds of forest to roam. We would walk for miles, discovering nature. It was so peaceful and calm, Tyler and I had been communicating much more than we did in Toronto. All the stresses of high traffic driving were gone, and we had found peace.

This couldn't last forever, I thought, as most good things come to an end. However, I soaked it all up as much as I could. In the meantime, Tyler worked on getting his driver's license, and he started a school program. It was a special school, which allowed flexible learning options. I actively searched for work each day in my field of computers, and while doing this I realized there was not that much available in this small community. I discussed my options with Mavis, my step-mother, who was very resourceful, and she said, "Maybe you should start your own business." I loved that idea, and quickly took the initial steps to make that happen.

I signed myself up for a start your own business course, which could show you all the steps involved in making this happen. They would cover topics like writing a business plan, finding capital required, and promoting or marketing your business. It was a six-week intensive course that would soon take me to a new direction in my life. I had a dream for years, to open and run a spiritual development center for people like myself, who struggled as a youth, and who had major things happen to them that affected their lives. I had always felt there was some higher purpose for my life that God wanted me to do. I believed this was the reason I had gone through such terrible things as a child. I was strong enough to get out of it using many techniques and resources along the way. What better way to give back to my community and share and assist people to succeed.

Now I not only had the teaching skills, but also the spiritual ability as well. I could teach them motivational skills that I learned from Anthony Robbins, meditation, relaxation, which I learned from the church, but most importantly, I had real life skills from my own experiences on the streets. I was so excited about this new venture, nothing could stop me now. I eagerly attended the program, completing all the assignments with ease. Then a twist was put into my plan; a bump in the road, as you might say.

Once everyone had all their facts and plans in writing, it was time for a group critique. I was never open to much criticism in my life; I usually blocked it out, as it was the only way I could survive most times, by believing I could do anything. However, I had done everything so far, and knew this was an important step in the process, and I must get a grip. When it was my turn, I excitedly presented all of my ideas and plans. The group then asked questions, as if they were the consumer. Most of the answers flowed quite easily until they asked this question: "If someone has a troubled past and while meditating, etc., you touched an area that upset them and they start freaking out, what qualifications do you have to help them?"

I responded with my life skills. The group and instructor said, "Without a psychology degree or counseling certificate there may be liabilities involved. The community would be hesitant to put their trust in you based on your lack of qualifications." I was devastated. This had really put a damper on my plans. They were right. "Who did I think I was?" kept running through my head.

In all honesty, they did not want anyone to fail with their plans. In life and business you will always face adversity. What you need to do is, come up with a plan to fix it, or surpass it. They suggested more training for me in counseling. I said, "This will take too long and lots of money," which I did not have. Again the group had a suggestion, to take a counseling course that took only six months, and there were programs where the government would pay. I was relieved, now able to see that my plan could still work. So this is where the next part of my journey took me.

***

I signed up and got government assistance to become a certified counselor. Still believing this would take me one step closer to completing my business plan, I happily took the journey to class each day. It was very intensive. Basically a two-year course packed into six months. They covered theory and hands-on practice in the following areas: child and adolescent counseling skills, sexual abuse, treatment and psychiatric disorders, couples and family counseling, substance abuse, and loss and grief support.

Strangely enough I loved school; I always had. The only problem when I was young was getting along with my peers. Don't get me wrong, I did have some friends in school, but not many. I always had this feeling of being different from everyone else; an outsider you might say. Now looking back, it probably had a lot to do with what I had experienced as a child. Most people in school had two-parent homes, and I never knew of anyone who had been molested, or who had watched their mother slash someone's head open, never mind the Children's Aid issues. It didn't help that I had moved to new schools all the time either.

Then as a teenager, after I had been forced to move out on the streets, I still wanted to go to school. I first called the Army, hoping they would let me in. I had heard they provided school with their specialist programs. I was denied, due to not having my grade twelve, and the fact that I was only fourteen at the time. By this time, my self-confidence was shot and the fear took over. So the day I walked over to the high school near my mother's house and saw all the kids, I realized, I could not do it, for fear of not fitting in. As an adult it was different. It opened brand-new doors for me. The adults wouldn't tease me or be mean to me. They also came with lots of baggage themselves by this time, so they really weren't any different in my eyes. Besides, after Roger's abuse, I had regained my self-confidence and strength, and knew I could do anything I set my mind to. School or education would always be a part of that.

At the first counseling class when the teacher did an overview of the months to come, she described one line in particular that I remembered, it read something like this: "Each person has ten free counseling sessions for themselves if needed." The teacher explained that by doing this course many cooped up feelings that a person had, may reveal themselves. Of course I did not think this applied to me, since I felt I had already dealt with my issues, otherwise how could I have made it this far in my life?

The course was grueling and totally intense, many long

hours of study in class, with lots of assignments to do at home. But I was determined that no matter how hard it got, I would complete it.

While I read through my counseling course notes and assignments, many memories I had forgotten about were brought to life. I had always felt that the sexual abuse section was the only area I would need to address in counseling. However, I soon found out there were many other areas in my life that were affected.

Attending this course was like an emotional operation being performed each day. I had no idea that I had any past issues to deal with. However, I soon found out there were many unresolved issues, where things could have been dealt with differently, had I known.

It started with the section on child and adolescent counseling. One of the first exercises in this course was to draw a chino gram or a family map. Twenty-five percent of people are kinesthetic, and seventy-five percent are visual. With the chino gram you basically are drawing a series of circles and squares, each one representing yourself and other people in your life, then adding various lines connecting them. Dependent upon the relationship between the parties (squares and circles), would decide what type of line was drawn between them. For example, a straight line meant good, a squiggly line not so good, and the dashed line was distant.

As I considered which lines to use, it forced me to focus on and analyze these relationships, doing exactly what it was supposed to do by bringing all kinds of memories to the forefront. I could feel all of the emotions that came with them while my mind was fighting to repress them, my body began to react. I looked around and took a deep breath, as I saw all the strange faces in the room. I did not want to show my weaknesses to these people, and quickly held it back. I put my thoughts elsewhere and quickly did the exercise.

When it was over, I began daydreaming, staring blankly into space, and frantically scribbling on my page. It was a constant, internal battle happening, while I waited for everyone else to finish their exercise. But it was not over yet. The next step was for each person to explain to the class the details of their chino gram. "Shit," I thought, "I was doing so well at holding back on my feelings." I was not sure if I could maintain this strength if I had to keep delving into my past like this.

I contained my emotions and when it was my turn to describe my drawing I did so professionally, as if it was someone else's, not letting any personal thoughts into the picture. I was relieved when it was over, and happy that I did not let anyone see that painful side. All I wanted was to move on to the next exercise so it would all go away, not realizing that the next diagram we would have to draw was my lifeline, starting from birth until present. Basically drawing a straight line and putting notches in it to represent each stage of my life and what was happening at that time.

It was difficult at first, especially when I got to my teen years. It was all a blur; I could not remember what, if any, significant things happened during that time. I don't think I couldn't really; it was just that I was not prepared to go there. Oh, I forgot to mention, when the teacher asked the students to do the chino gram and lifeline, she said to do it based upon an issue you want to deal with. I wrote in my notes "men." Later when I went home to complete my exercise I was able to fill in some of the blanks on my lifeline...the blurred areas. It seemed easier for me when I was alone because I did not have to keep my guard up.

Some days I did not think I would get through this course. Throughout all of this, I not only practiced being a counselor in exercises, but everyone also had to be the patient. I had promised myself after the incident with the counselor in my group home, that I would never see another counselor again. I swore no one would break into my heart and shatter it.

That was a pretty powerful belief system I had carried with me over the years. So even if people wanted to help me, I wouldn't let them in. Anthony Robbins talked about belief systems through his teachings. He strongly believed it was the key to making changes in your life. Only problem was my interpretation of this was, not to think about them, and to move on.

This understanding wasn't working for me because I carried a deep anger and hatred for all men, except my son. And my son would become angry and hateful too. Not only from what he had witnessed as a child, but also the comments I would blurt out in order to protect myself and give me strength. I would say over and over again, "All men are assholes and no good." I never, ever, meant this in reference to my son, but I believe now that maybe this contributed to his low self-esteem growing up.

Oh the guilt you harbor over your actions with raising your child. I don't think there is a caring parent out there that doesn't feel some sort of guilt for some area of their child's life. If only there was a handbook to follow, then maybe things would be different. Unfortunately, because each person is different, it is virtually impossible to address everything you will face, as many authors and readers have found out. In my opinion, every person should go through some type of awakening exercises after adolescence, combining counseling and meditation group discussions, to find out who they are, your likes and dislikes, and to obtain some coping mechanisms to take you through life. Then once you feel complete within yourself, bring in the relationship; just a thought. Really no one has the magic answer.

Back to me and my counseling classes. I survived child and adolescent counseling. Now moving on to cognitive behavior counseling, this area dealt a lot with cause-and-effect and classic conditioning. Basically why people do things, what happens when they do them, and the conditioning that went on in order to program this behavior or belief system in their minds. Again, all of these areas were discussed in the Anthony Robbins series of tapes. But if the door is locked and you won't let anyone in, how can there be change? I did not see this was the case with me.

As the course went on I made comparisons to my life and how I was conditioned, what my triggers were, and the causes and effects of the actions of the people around me. This was all very enlightening, but how could I fix things for everyone. You see, that was my forte. I loved helping people to succeed. Passing on the strength I had to take me through my own life. Although not very patient with those people who did not want to help themselves, I did my best to surround myself with strong, positive people, or people who have the willpower to change, but just didn't know how, and needed guidance. These were some of the traits that made me a good teacher.

This next section of the course was the most difficult one, as it covered sexual abuse. Again I thought I had dealt with this previously by bringing it out in the open. I remembered how difficult it was for the words to come out of my mouth. My face turned red, and burned with shame, when I told my family I was molested. By speaking out to my father, and the rest of my family who were there, I soon realized that I was not alone when my sister also mentioned that similar things had happen to her at that house. There really is something to say about group therapy. There is nothing worse than feeling you are so different from others that such things would happen to you only. But by listening to others share their experiences, you gain a sense of comfort and strength in knowing that you are not alone. I shared my experience with thousands of people after that, each time feeling just a little bit better. I also found out by doing this how many people out there have had some pretty rotten things happen to them too.

These were some of the reasons I thought it was over, in my mind. As the course content was described, I started experiencing many of the forms of recurring trauma, like flashbacks, numbing, avoidance, disassociation, emotional shutdown or psychic numbing, and triggers. These were all hyper-arousal symptoms of PTSD. I began to realize that these were many of the tools I was using to cope all these years. I tried my hardest to listen to the course content, but found myself disassociating, staring into space, daydreaming of nicer things, and then coming back into focus when my body had taken control of its vitals. I could only remain in focus for short periods of time, until yet another trigger would put me back to sexually uncomfortable places.

Not just the first incident but the many others that occurred in my teen to adult years would surface. I had come to believe this was normal behavior to treat me this way. But after listening to this section of the course, I realized it was not. Then the guilt set in, and the blame, that maybe it was my fault. It was like a ripple effect moving its way down to how I reared my son. The emotions were running high in the classroom, as I was not the only one who had bad experiences sexually. I continued to use all the techniques I could to control myself from expressing any of my weaknesses to my classmates or instructor.

It was too much; I could not contain myself anymore. I left the room to go down to my car and began bawling as I lit up a smoke. I scanned my brain looking for ways to make these feelings go away so I could go back to class. For some reason, this time, there was no way out, unless I had help. I had heard earlier that day that the school would not honor the ten free counseling sessions with Shelley the instructor. This was the only person I felt some connection with and could not possibly bring myself to see someone else at this point. There was no way out. I pleaded with God to help me make this pain go away.

Moments later Shelley arrived outside my car door and asked if I was okay. I quickly maintained my strength, as I always did around others and said, "I am fine." But Shelley was an expert in this area and knew otherwise. Her soft-spoken, caring voice, kept breaking down the barriers I had up, and the tears began to flow again. Shelley assured me that, even though the school would not pay her to counsel me, she would do it anyway, for free.

"Oh no," I said, "I could not possibly ask you to do that."

Shelley then said, "I am offering and I don't mind. I want to do it. Don't worry about the money."

But I did not like to accept charity from people, it had something to do with IOU and I didn't want that. When Shelley realized this was an issue for me she said, "Someday you can pay me back if you want." This would work, I thought, because no matter how long it took me, I would never forget this gesture, and would definitely pay her back someday. Shelley spent an extra few minutes calming me down and then we returned to class.

At that point my life would change once again, bringing me to a new level. These were deep-rooted issues I had never dealt with, and now I had someone I really trusted to help me through them. I ended up completing the course with honors, while attending sessions with Shelley on the weekend. The sessions even continued a few weeks past the course completion until the tenth one was over. A lot of progress was made during that time. I realized I did not really love myself. I felt a sense of inadequacy, stemming from all of my childhood experiences. Together we worked on recognizing what these associations were, and the steps to deal with the triggers.

I had a fear that I would not be able to go at this alone, but knew I must leave the British Columbia. I had spent months in tears, depressed and lonely. When my brother realized this, he convinced me that things would be better if I came to Edmonton where he was. I had agreed and made all of the arrangements to move once class was completed.

Even though we had made a lot of progress, Shelley still recommended I continue with my therapy. With all the trust issues I knew this would not be possible with someone else. It was a sad day when the last session was over and we had to say goodbye.

CHAPTER FIFTEEN

TRUE LOVE

When I arrived in Edmonton, I looked for work in the field of computers and training, like I had successfully done in Toronto. There was nothing available, so I took a dead-end job as an assistant for a delivery company called Excel, making ten dollars an hour through a temp agency. With barely enough to live on, however, I made it work.

It was summer 2002 and I was still feeling depressed and lonely, although I did feel somewhat better being away from British Columbia and near my brother. It had been several months now for me working at Excel and Tyler was more out of control then he had ever been. He had met some friends and seemed to be all drugged up most of the time. I insisted he find work, since he was not going to school. He said he would and that he was looking, but I knew otherwise, since he was usually playing Nintendo and could not remember where he applied.

The situation got progressively worse and Tyler became more and more verbally abusive to me, even to the point of throwing objects. Nothing hit or hurt me, but the stress was devastating, and now I feared for my safety. When my brother got wind of the situation he pressured me to do something about it. I did not want to put my son on the street and did not know what else to do. So my brother, understanding that, suggested I get him an apartment, pay his first and last month's rent and move him out. Then he would have to find a job in order to survive. Well, this backfired.

I rented Tyler an apartment by convincing the landlord he would be a good tenant, packed his stuff, and moved him out. This was not an easy thing for me to do. This was my baby and I felt I was abandoning him. Even though I knew it was necessary, it still did not feel any easier for me to do it, you know "the tough love theory." Tyler lied to me when I would call; telling me he found a job and everything was okay. I soon realized by his voice that things were not okay. Also, the landlord kept calling, saying that my son was having loud parties and lots of people coming in and out.

I decided I would go and see for myself what was going on and showed up at his door. Tyler answered wide-eyed, wearing high winter boots in the middle of the summer, with a large hunting knife stuffed in the side. He paced frantically, looking all around, as if completely paranoid. He let me in after scanning the area for perpetrators then he closed the door behind us. I was in complete shock. The place was an absolute disaster, clothes all over the floor, a hole in the wall, a melted cutting board on the stove, with black smoke marks under the cabinet above. What a disgrace. When I freaked out asking Tyler, "What is going on?" he made no sense, although he did say he had everything under control. We ended up getting in an argument and I went home.

Devastated, I called my brother to explain what I found. Not getting much sympathy there, I decided to call my sister Jenny. Jenny, the caring person she was, said, "You have to get him out of there," which was exactly the confirmation I needed. I also felt I could not leave him in this state. I called Tyler and told him he was coming home and I would be there later.

Let me first explain the reason the landlady said there were so many people in and out of there. I found out that Tyler felt bad for the people living on the street, so he would invite them in to stay. That was how he got into the heavier drugs, which I later found out was crystal meth.

Tyler agreed to come home, but was worried for the people staying there. He did not want them getting mad at him, or have nowhere to stay. He seemed quite afraid. At this point, I was psychotic and didn't care. When I showed up I had a scowl on that would scare anyone off. Tyler was very familiar with this look and became nervous of what I might do, so he quickly introduced the guy that was there to me, and frantically started putting his things in garbage bags. The man he introduced was named "Bulldog." Can you imagine that? He looked like a bulldog too. Crushed face, bald head, and somewhat muscular. Like I said, I was psychotic at this point and was not afraid of anyone. I glared at Bulldog with a look that could kill, as he bragged about the hole in the wall and laughed. I asked him, "Did you do that?" Before he could answer, Tyler, knowing where I was going with this said, "I am ready, let's go, Mom," and pulled me out the door.

Upon leaving I stopped by the landlord's apartment and said, "Tyler is now out, you can call the police to get whoever is left in there out. I will be back to clean up."

When I returned a few days later to clean up, I was even more disgusted when I got to the bathroom, which I had not seen the first time. There was no toilet seat, it was completely plugged with anything and everything you could imagine, the counter and floors were filthy dirty, with cigarette butts and drug paraphernalia everywhere. The worst part was, the bathtub and walls were covered in vomit and excrement.

Before I attempted to clean it, the landlady showed up and said, "Don't clean this please, just leave, and don't bring your son back, I will clean it." I apologized for everything my son had put her through. The landlady accepted the apology and thanked me for getting him out. It was a long, drawn-out process to get Tyler off the drugs after that, but somehow my continued love for him prevailed, and he stopped using the meth. However, the verbal abuse continued and he refused to get help by seeing a counselor, whom I made calls to set up.

So again, I was forced to initiate more tough love. I told Tyler, if he did not find work in three months, he would have to move. Of course he did not ever try and continued mouthing off. So I packed a green garbage bag of clothes, put him in the car, and dropped him off at the shelter, hoping he would be forced to get some help there. Tyler was terrified and somehow made his way back to my house later that day, pleading to use the phone, saying he would call a friend in British Columbia to go there.

That is what he did. His old girlfriend who adored him convinced her parents to pay for his flight and take him in, with the promise from Tyler that he would find a job and pay them back. Off he went, and I was overwhelmed with grief from losing him but at the same time, hopeful this change would be good. In the meantime, my brother hired me part-time to work with him in his show home. He was a new home sales consultant, and making big bucks. He said, "I will teach you what I know, and maybe you can find a job doing the same thing." So I listened and learned all that I could, and convinced myself I could do this. Applying all the techniques I learned from Anthony Robbins training like "change your belief system," "create certainty," "that you can do anything you set your mind to." That is exactly what I did.

***

I became extremely competent in my sales ability, and applied for any new home sales position that came up. Finally after numerous resumes and calls, I had several interviews with the top salesperson in Edmonton. He offered to hire me as an assistant/area manager. However, he was not willing to pay very much. After negotiating and renegotiating, with my brother coaching me from behind, I eventually turned him down. Continuing on, still feeling confident I would eventually succeed, I applied at Royal Paris Homes. My brother had warned me that the owner/manager had a very bad reputation in the industry. Many salespeople had quit or been fired for not conforming to his ruthless demands.

Although this was the case, I knew I had a special knack for dealing with difficult people. When I taught for the Government of Ontario, I had been chosen many times to take over classes of difficult students. I remembered one class specifically. It was a group of social workers from a bad area of Toronto. The instructor that was teaching them was a very strict, old army guy. He did not take any shit. But this crew was totally out of control. To start off they were dressed like the welfare recipients they gave checks to, black leather pants, chains hanging from the hip, nose and eyebrow piercings, wild hair, it was ludicrous. They were so obnoxious and rude, turning their backs to the instructor. One of them came back from class late after break, which is never okay with the military people, who are so structured. And to top it all off, he said to the instructor "fuck off" when confronted. That was the last straw for that teacher. He left the class and told management that he would no longer teach that class.

So here the students, out of control, were now feeling they had won the battle once he walked out. Management knew I had a pretty strong character, and I had received many positive reviews from students, so they asked me to take over. I enjoyed challenges, I loved proving to myself and others that anything was possible, so I eagerly agreed to take over.

I remembered that day vividly. It was like one of those movies I'd watched before, where a teacher went into a school in the Bronx, and changed the lives of the emotionally destructive teens. My heart raced as I approached the classroom door. Even though the nervous adrenaline was flowing through my body, I did not for one second doubt that this was possible. I took a deep breath and forged through the door. It was exactly as the movies, except these were young adults. Many of them with their backs turned, playing some kind of boom box in the back of the room. The rest of them sitting slouched, displaying complete attitude, while chatting loudly amongst themselves.

As I attempted to introduce myself, no one acknowledged. They continued to have their own conversation, as if I did not exist. I very calmly walked in front of my desk, leaned against it and crossed my arms, as if to say, "I will not tolerate this." I smiled slyly and said, "It's okay. I hope you all brought your sleeping bags, because we can stay here all night if you like." I could see even though they did not look up, that they heard what I said. I then went completely quiet, and sat there staring out at all of them. Now, I don't know if you remember ever having felt or seen someone staring at you from afar, but it is extremely uncomfortable. The more the students tried to ignore me, the more they felt the uneasy feeling of my eyes glaring at them from behind.

After about fifteen minutes passed, some of them just couldn't take it anymore and turned towards me prepared to listen. Others asked questions like, "What are we going to learn today?" as the rest of the class continued to be disruptive in the back. I only responded with, "Once I have the whole class's attention, we will start." As I spoke, a few in the back looked up, glaring with attitude. I looked directly in their eyes and said, "Those of you who don't want to be here, can leave. Here is the door."

They quickly responded saying, "We were forced to do this course, or we will lose our jobs." I responded with, "Then you are going to need to pay attention, because there are other people here who want to learn." I began to engage them in conversation asking questions about things they knew, and complimenting them on their knowledge and abilities. You see I knew this fine art of making people feel good. This was all I ever wanted growing up, was to hear my teachers, family or friends say, "You did a good job." To hear my father say, "I am proud of you." Those words did not come from him until much later in life, long after it was due. My sister, however, always told me I could do anything, and she was proud of me. That was the strength that carried me through those tough years. This technique I used in my teaching was very successful. I engaged all the students in conversation, and rewarded them for their efforts, through my words and actions. I successfully turned that out-of-control class into a team of respectful students resulting in rave reviews. No one could believe it except me. I had shared with my students a kindness, caring, and respect, that they all needed.

I became a very successful teacher, even though I was chosen in the second batch of instructors, because the hiring company was short staffed. The reason that happened was because management was looking at credentials. I did not have a university degree, but I sure knew how to handle people, and do my job well; better than those that did have a degree. Later I realized these were some of the teachings of Anthony Robbins, and I knew how good it made me feel, so why wouldn't it work with others.

***

For all of these reasons, I decided to go for it and applied at Royal Paris Homes. At first I had an interview with the current sales manager, Darlene, at Boston Pizza. The interview went really well, she said she would be in touch in a few days. When that didn't happen, I did a follow up call and found that Darlene had since then quit her job. She didn't say much as to why, only that she would be pursuing a new venture. Darlene advised me to call Damien, the owner, directly, because she had already told him about me and he would be expecting the call.

So I made the call and when the two of us met, we connected like two peas in a pod. We talked for over an hour and a half, about anything and everything. By the time we were done, I was hired, and going to be placed in his best show home.

He taught me everything he knew first hand. I absorbed it all like a sponge, and later became his top salesperson, earning a six-figure income for several years. I was on top of the world, combining all I had learned about housing with my teaching techniques and my honest, up front personality. The customers loved me and trusted me with the biggest purchase of their life. In addition, they sent hundreds of referrals my way.

I was ecstatic, and I knew how to handle Damien. Within the first few months, even though I was extremely happy with my career and the money I was making, there was still something missing. I was lonely without someone else in my life to share it with; a lover and companion. For many years I had told myself that I didn't need a man, and that all men are assholes. But since British Columbia, those thoughts did not come up as often, mostly the feeling of being isolated and lonely. Career and money were much easier for me to accomplish. All I had to do was focus on it hard enough, take the necessary steps, and it would happen. With men it was different, I thought. I had literally eliminated them from my mind, in order to survive, building up a wall of protection, which came partially tumbling down with the counseling.

I realized a lot of my feelings about men stemmed from my childhood, and the belief system that was instilled in me. There was something missing to balance my life. It was having someone to share it with, I thought.

***

On July 6, 2004 at 11:06 p.m. I was meditating and this unusual message came forth.

He will come; think about your man and he will come. Put the thought forth – so it is done.

He will be strong; masculine, yet feminine at heart. He will be gentle yet strong. Somewhat intelligent, yet not too much as to overpower, as you want to feel special and important to the one who chooses you. Yes, don't be in shock, he will choose you. He will win your heart by leaps and bounds. You will just know there is no fear. You will just know this is right. All you have learned has brought you this far. Without it, this day would never come.

What else can we tell you about him? Brown hair, deep brown eyes like yours, bedroom eyes, when you look into them, you are hypnotized. It's almost electrical. He will be funny and make you laugh. He will also find you funny, with almost a silliness to it.

He will have a good body, with strong arms, and a nice butt, very sexy in blue jeans, great teeth, with a nice smile. Very sexy, almost innocent like.

He will believe in what you believe in. He will be intrigued with all you have to say.

He will have his own money, and will always insist upon treating you. You are his lady – he must protect and save you from your despair.

He will have a genuine love for your son, and your son with him. There will be no jealousy, only camaraderie.

He will be there when you need him. He will cleanse your soul of any impurities, and then and only then, will you be truly balanced. You go, girl.

As excited as I was to hear that message, I soon forgot it existed when Mister Right did not suddenly appear. Not until several years later, after all of the activities happened before me, did I find this writing in an old notebook on the shelf. Interesting...

Around the beginning of August I signed up for an online dating service called "Lava Life." I carefully thought out the detailed description of who I was. My likes, dislikes, needs and wants. Here is what it said...

I am an independent, career oriented woman. I believe that everything happens for a reason. I am not afraid to take risks. The gym is one of my favorite pastimes when I make time. I love to play pool, dance, or just sit up all night and have stimulating conversations about everything that comes to mind. I like to have fun and laugh sometimes at the silly stuff. Just moved to Edmonton one year ago and I haven't met that special man to spend time with.

I do not have any lists or 'don't wants' in a man. I believe that everyone has their own special qualities, that when ignited can come to life. So if you are one of these men with a "list", then I will probably not fit all of your criteria.

The core though is honesty, communication, gentle yet strong, someone with a good heart, who will not bring any more sadness into my life. Someone who will love me for who I am, all of me.

Although I am very passionate...If you are looking for a roll in the hay - and that's all - then I am sure there are many women on here who can give you what you need, but it will not be me, sorry.

I live a very positive lifestyle - never dwelling on negativity - always looking for the positive in every situation. Some say my head is in the clouds because I still believe in true love and romance. My name tells you there is more to this profile than meets the eye (online name: uneekone).

If some or all of what I have said intrigues you, then send me a smile. If I respond, I am also intrigued. If I do not - please accept my deep gratitude for making me feel special today. Thank you!

I have msn but need a few minutes of your time with your pictures (not shallow - visual connection) to move to the next level. It is only fair since I have displayed mine.

Romance me and I'm yours!

I added a few photos and logged in. At first I was hopeful I would find myself the perfect mate. When I received my first message from someone I was excited. However, after about five dates with different eligible bachelors, my excitement soon dwindled.

I began logging on only to pass the time. Until one night after I logged in a message popped up on screen. "Hello, I just saw your profile and I would like to chat with you." The first thing I always did before agreeing to speak with anyone online was to check out their profile to see if they met my minimum criteria. When I looked to see what this guy was all about and hopefully to catch a glimpse of him in a photo, there wasn't much there. There was his age; a few years older than me, hair color, eye color, height five foot ten; this was a minimum requirement of mine, and a few of his interests. For example casino, drink socially only, has kids, does not want anymore, camping – not sure about this one, I thought, travel, playing pool. Oh and also, how much money he made was another important factor, one hundred thousand plus per year.

After seeing that he had some of the same interests, I was a bit intrigued. However, I was very nervous that he had no picture on his profile. This was usually a good indication that he was not good looking, or had some weight or teeth issues. So of course, I responded to him letting him know that he had limited information about himself online, and that it was imperative that I see a picture. Now I know that sounds like I was only concerned about looks, but that wasn't the case. Yes, part of it was that I did want to see if I was attracted to him, and whether he had good teeth, as this was something I had decided would be important. However, another reason to see his photo was to see if I sensed anything good or bad about him. Remember, I mentioned earlier about my psychic abilities; well, I usually could tell by looking at someone if they were a creep, or at least I thought I could.

Anyway, he quickly replied, telling me he had just set his account up, and it takes a couple of days to get approval, and that was why his information was not complete. He promised he would provide me with any information and pictures I wanted, while waiting for the approval. I agreed to chat with him only online, for now. First thing I asked for was the photo, which he emailed to me right away. I was not too enthusiastic and quite frankly was a bit suspicious of the fact that there was only basic information listed on him, but I really did not have anything better to do that night.

Arriving in my inbox was the photo. I quickly opened it, eager to see who this person was. Here is this guy sporting some tight blue jeans, a lumber jacket, and a hat against an autumn setting background, with leaves strewn about all over the ground. To top it all off, he is demonstrating one of the top hot male activities, "chopping wood with a big axe." Not bad, I thought, the picture is a bit far away, but so far I was not turned off. Even though he was smiling, I could not see a close up of his teeth. This was really important since the last guy I went on a date with surprised me with a full mouth of rotten, brown, green, yellow teeth with severely bad breath to match. Definitely an experience I wanted to avoid in the future.

I insisted that Rick send me a photo where I could see his teeth. The guy probably thought I was nuts, but he appeased me anyway. The second photo was not perfect, but it was enough that I could see his teeth were ok. Once that was over, I then drilled him with hundreds of questions, from what do you do for a living, to revealing his horoscope sun sign. This interrogation went on for days through the online chat and then progressed to msn messenger, so that Rick did not have to continue paying for the chat service on Lava Life.

I was looking for all possible reasons not to date this guy, simply for my own protection. It was also a great big test, actually. I knew how difficult I could be in a relationship, due to my excessive baggage I carried along with me, so if the guy can't take the slightest bit of adversity, then he is probably not the right guy for me. It is a good thing that Rick was so smitten, as he truly thought I was just trying to get to know him; meanwhile I was searching for reasons to put him on the "shit list" with the rest of the men.

In all honesty, I had taken down several bricks after my counseling sessions in British Columbia, but there were so many that I didn't think they would all ever be removed completely. Well Rick had passed all the tests with flying colors so far. He was not giving me any reason to avoid him. And I was truly enjoying my conversations with him. We would chat for hours online, about anything and everything, and then eventually it progressed to the phone. Even after the initial discomfort was over, of hearing each other's voices, we still continued to talk, night after night.

Rick was eager to meet me in person and kept asking me over and over again for a date. I had a lot on my plate; I was selling new homes, with many nights working overtime. It was at the early stages of the housing boom and I absolutely loved my job. I loved connecting with my customers and teaching them what they needed to know to purchase their home. I was making huge money and feeling pretty good being independent. I was not sure I wanted this type of man, who seemed to want me all the time in my life. Yes, I really enjoyed speaking with him, but I definitely did not want someone hanging on to my skirt, while I explored the world. Maybe enjoy a night here and there, but that was it. It seemed like Rick wanted more than that, which was indicated by his persistence.

He said, "Do you want to go to dinner?" I said, "I am busy," "How about lunch," he persisted. "I am busy," I continued to push him away. "What about tomorrow, are you free?" "No," I replied. "When will you be free?" he asked with exhaustion in his voice, "I really want to meet you." Finally I had an idea. "Well, if you really want to see me you can meet me at Costco (which is a store) in the morning." Rick said, "Costco, you want me to meet you at Costco?"

I said, "Yes, I have shit to do, and I am busy, so if you want to meet me, then Costco is where I will be. Rick jumped at the opportunity, and didn't care where it was at this point, and agreed to meet me at nine-thirty a.m. when the store opened.

Rick had arrived early, eager to meet this mysterious woman, whom he had been talking to for hours upon hours, and waited patiently in the parking lot for me to arrive. We described each of our vehicles, and of course we had seen pictures the day before, so we knew how to find each other a little easier.

I came racing into the parking lot in my red, standard, Honda Civic, and quickly located Ricks' four-by-four Trailblazer and pulled into the spot beside him. Well, after that erratic entry, if Rick wasn't terrified enough before, he certainly was now. He must have thought, "This woman is a maniac." Somehow for Rick, this was exciting, as he led a fairly simple life up to now.

My heart raced, as I saw this hot looking guy get out of his vehicle. He was wearing tight blue jeans and a black jacket and he looked great. I was not about to let him know this, so I did everything I could to keep my cool. Rick spoke first and said, "Are you Michele?"

"Yes, this is me," I replied, and we shook hands and proceeded to go into the store. It was really awkward to meet a stranger this way, even though we had talked on the phone, we really didn't know each other, so the store thing was good because we could keep busy, while subtly flirting with each other.

The first part was good, but I wasn't finished with my testing yet. It seemed there was more that poor Rick would have to endure, before getting to the next step. I noticed there was a manager in the produce department, and I had recently had some issues with the produce, and decided today was the day. I politely asked Rick to stay where he was, and told him I had something to deal with that he might not want to see. At least I warned him. I walked over to the produce manager and tore a strip out of him. I said, "Every time I buy fruit here I get them home and they are bad, what kind of an operation are you running?" and on and on and on.

Eventually, the produce manager said I could keep my receipt next time and return them to the store and they would refund my money. With a snarly comment I said, "That is not good enough, you should not be selling rotten fruit in the first place." As I turned to walk away, I bumped smack dab into Rick, who was observing my behavior the whole time. Well, I thought fine then, "If he wants to see what I am like, then I have nothing to hide."

If Rick were going to walk away, now would be the time. But no, he still wanted more of me. Now I figured, if this guy first of all would be willing to meet me at a store, shop comfortably, and listen to me abuse the produce manager, maybe he is up to handling me at my worst. And a few more bricks came tumbling down from my wall.

Rick and I hung out shopping all morning looking for a webcam for our computers. We went from store to store, and Rick passed another test on the way, just being a passenger in my vehicle, without showing any fear. You see I drove like "Mario Andretti," the racecar driver, cutting corners, flying in and out of traffic to get in the lead. Rick handled it well, and didn't even use the "holy shit bars."

It was time for me to go to work and neither one of us wanted to separate. We just couldn't get enough of each other. Before I dropped Rick back off to his car, I stopped at my place, to change into my work clothes. Unbelievably comfortable so soon, that I would even consider bringing a stranger to my house. But something was different this time; it felt so natural, as if we had known each other for years. I wasn't about to analyze it, I just thought, "What the hell, let's just go with the flow."

Do you think this was finally my opportunity to find true love and happiness, after all I had been through with men, or was it too good to be true? Several months before, I had written out a wish list of the qualities I wanted in a man. Rick matched all of them, to a tee. It was like a dream come true.

I worked all day at the show home, constantly thinking about this mysterious man I just met, hoping he would contact me again, but preparing myself, just in case he didn't. "It's ok if he doesn't call; there are plenty of fish in the sea, and I will be ok," I said to myself.

You see the plan was, that Rick would return later that night for a date. For some reason, this day felt the longest ever, with me constantly checking the time to see if it was five o'clock. When it arrived, I couldn't get out of there fast enough to scoot home and get ready for my date that night.

Rick was just as eager to connect with me again, except he was at home thinking about me all day, without anything to distract him. He had all day to plan what he would do that night to intrigue me. Not wanting to be late, Rick left home very early. He even showed up a half hour before, and waited in his car parked down the street. He did not want me to think he was too eager, or be mad at him for showing up at my door when I did not have time to get ready. "So thoughtful of him to consider my feelings that way," I thought afterwards when I found out.

At exactly six-thirty p.m., Rick knocked on the door to pick me up for our date, with flowers in hand and a box of white chocolates, which he had found out over our talks, was my favorite type. I opened the door and there he was, looking even better then I remembered in his tight blue jeans. The smell of his cologne mixed with his body chemistry, hypnotized me and I almost melted right there where I stood. Quickly taking a deep breath to contain my composure, I greeted him and invited him in to wait, while I completed a few final tasks.

I could feel his eyes on me the whole time, making shivers crawl up my arms. I was pretty good at pretending to be standoffish and in control, so as not to let anyone think they had control of me. So that is exactly what I did, carrying on nonchalantly, while Rick watched me.

Rick took me out to dinner and the casino that night, both things I loved to do. However, my focus was on Rick and the energy I felt, just being near him. We took every opportunity we could to be close to each other, while jumping back to catch our breath every few minutes or so.

Once the evening was over, Rick took me back to my house, and I politely invited him in. We sat on the couch and talked for hours, wanting to savor each moment we had together, as if it was our first and last. When the energy was so great in the room, Rick politely asked me permission to give me a kiss. Well, I was completely blown away. No one had ever asked me that before. Usually they just took it or tried to take it from me. I completely melted in his arms, and shyly agreed to his request. And the rest is history.

The bond was so great; it felt as if we had known each other forever. I had finally met my soul mate, someone to share my life with. Rick was a special person, who would show me the love I so desperately yearned for all those years. He brought peace to my heart in so many ways. Tyler loved him too, just like he was his own father, with no jealousy like the others I had been with. Even my family was over the moon about him, after they got over the fact that we were taking things too quickly for their liking. But Rick and I knew it was right, and we didn't care what anyone else thought. After so many years of loneliness, sadness and abuse, we both decided we would take that leap of faith, without anyone else's approval. If I learned anything over the years it was that life is short, and you must capture and appreciate every moment of your life now, because when the time has passed, you cannot get it back.

Within a few weeks Rick moved in, and several months later we bought a brand new home and have been together ever since. Yes, it is like a fairy tale. And no, it has not always been perfect, but that wouldn't be very much fun, would it? But we are living happily ever after.

Tyler is now married common law, and has a son of his own. He has come to realize the many sacrifices I made for him over the years, and has spent countless hours expressing his regret for the trouble he caused me, and gratitude for the life I gave him. Not a day goes by where we don't call each other to say, "I love you." I am very proud of him that he was able to pull himself out of the many situations he was in, and to make something of himself. He turned out to be a very admirable young man. As a husband now, he shows great respect for women and how to treat them, which was one thing I always hoped he would learn from the things he heard and saw in my life experiences. This is the one type of love, the love for your child, that cannot be misinterpreted; not in my eyes, anyway. This was the bond, strength and purpose behind my motivation, to find true love. With the feeling of my child's unconditional love, and my sister's undivided belief system shown upon me, I was able to believe I was worthy of love. I knew in my heart that love existed in some form. This gave me the strength and determination to search beyond the boundaries of all I had known, past the misinterpretation of love, to seek out and find the freedom of my soul and to know that everything is possible.

These are my words of wisdom I will leave you with. "Ask and you shall receive. Believe so that you know it is possible. Accept it as if it was already yours when it arrives. And savor each moment after that, because when it all ends, this is what will remain in your heart, true love." Most importantly, "Love yourself, because no matter what has happened in your life, you are worthy."

FROM THE AUTHOR

Thank you very much for reading Fear Is Not An Option.

If you enjoyed it please take a moment to leave a review at your favorite online retailer such as Amazon USA or Amazon CA.

Most importantly if there is someone in your life who may be experiencing any form of abuse please show them love and kindness and let them know you are available if they need help.

I welcome contact from readers at my website, you can contact me, sign up for my newsletter to be notified of special events and new releases, join our SAVE ME campaign, read my blog and find me on social networking.

http://www.micheleanstead.com

Michele Anstead

45804792R00149

Made in the USA
Charleston, SC
02 September 2015